BIG METRIC NINJA FOODI COOKBOOK

Step-By-Step Ninja Foodi Recipes for Beginners and Advanced Users Using European Measurements

MYRTLE SCHAFF

© Copyright 2021 - All rights reserved.

ISBN: 9798473916492

The contents of this book may not be reproduced, duplicated or transmitted without direct written permission from the author.

Under no circumstances will any legal responsibility or blame be held against the publisher for any reparation, damages, or monetary loss due to the information herein, either directly or indirectly.

Legal Notice:

This book is copyright protected. This is only for personal use. You cannot amend, distribute, sell, use, quote or paraphrase any part of the content within this book without the consent of the author.

Disclaimer Notice:

Please note the information contained within this document is for educational and entertainment purposes only. Every attempt has been made to provide accurate, up to date and reliable information. No warranties of any kind are expressed or implied. Readers acknowledge that the author is not engaging in the rendering of legal, financial, medical or professional advice. The content of this book has been derived from various sources. Please consult a licensed professional before attempting any techniques outlined in this book.

By reading this document, the reader agrees that under no circumstances are is the author responsible for any losses, direct or indirect, which are incurred as a result of the use of information contained within this document, including, but not limited to, —errors, omissions, or inaccuracies

TABLE OF CONTENTS

Breakfast 6
   Coconut Oatmeal 7
   Almond Spice Oatmeal 8
   Carrot Cake Oats 9
   Morning Casserole 10
   Butter Chicken Bites 11
   Bangers & Mash 12
   Breakfast Broccoli Casserole 13
   Creamy Asparagus Soup 14
   Potato and Chorizo Frittata 15
   Curried Chickpea and Roasted Tomato 16
   Buttered Up Garlic and Fennel 17
   Broccoli and Scrambled Cheese Breakfast 18
   Asparagus Frittata 19
   Breakfast Muffins 20
   Curry Shredded Chicken 21
   Mashed Cauliflower Delight 22
   Great Brussels Bite 23

Poultry Recipes 24
   Chicken Bean Bake 25
   Shredded Salsa Chicken 26
   Barbecue Chicken 27
   Chicken Chile Verde 28
   Lemon and Chicken Extravaganza 29
   Lemon Chicken with Garlic 30
   Chicken Cacciatore 31
   Turkey Bean Chili 32
   Honey Teriyaki Chicken 33
   Chicken Balls in Melted Butter 34
   Summer Time Chicken Salad 35
   The Great Poblano Chicken Curry 36
   Chili Chicken Wings 37
   Cajun Turkey Breast 38

   Hearty Chicken Yum 39
   Lime Chicken Chili 40
   Chicken Piccata Pasta 41

Beef, Pork and Lamb 42
   Corned Beef and Cabbage 43
   Mustard Pork Chops 44
   Pork Carnitas 45
   Zesty Lamb Chops 46
   Beef Stroganoff 47
   Crispy Pork Carnitas 48
   Beef Chili 49
   Beef & Broccoli 50
   Rice Casserole and Minced Beef 51
   Pulled Pork 52
   Beefy Stew 53
   Lamb with Mint 54
   Sweet and Savoury Pork fillet steak 55
   Roasted Lamb Cutlet 56
   Pepper Garlic Pork Fillet Steak 57
   Simple Pressure-Cooked Lamb Meat ... 58
   Rosemary Anchovy Lamb 59

Fish and Sea Food 60
   Fish and Grits 61
   Sweet 'n Spicy Mahi-mahi 62
   Creamy Herb 'n Parm Salmon 63
   Pasta 'n Tuna Bake 64
   Shrimp Risotto 65
   Hearty Swordfish Meal 66
   Salmon Stew 67
   Chili Lime Salmon 68
   Salmon With Orange-ginger Sauce 69

Simple Fish Stew 70
Veggie Fish Soup 71
Garlic Sock-Eye Salmon 72
Cherry Tomato Mackerel 73
Shrimp Zoodles 74
Garlic And Lemon Prawn Delight 75
Breath-taking Cod Fillets 76
Flaky Fish with Ginger 77

Dessert Recipes 78

Meatloaf 79
Kale And Almonds Mix 80
Apple Pie Filling 81
Cheese Dredged Cauliflower Snack 82
Coconutty-blueberry Cake 83
Cauliflower Patties 84
Grape Jelly 85
Rice Pudding 86
Strawberry Chocolate Chip Mug Cake 87
Pound Cake 88

Onion and Smoky Mushroom Medley 89
Simple Treat of Garlic 90
Cauliflower Soup 91
Pumpkin Pie 92
Dried tomatoes 93
Paprika And Cabbage 94
Corn Dog Bites 95

Vegetable and Soup Recipes .. 96

Chili-quinoa 'n Black Bean Soup 97
Vegan Chili 98
Mashed Potatoes 99
Spinach and Chickpea Stew 100

Vegetable tart 101
Sweet sriracha carrots 102
Cauliflower puree with scallions 103
Chickpea and Potato Soup 104
Black beans in tomato sauce 105
Roasted veggie mix 106
Pressure Cooker Chicken Pot Pie Soup 107
Gentle and Simple Fish Stew 108
Creamy Early Morning Asparagus Soup 109
Beef Sausage Soup 110
Broccoli casserole 111

INTRODUCTION

Have you ever dreamed of a tool that could replace four or even five kitchen machines? I am sure that you are most likely familiar with the lack of space to put all the appliances in the kitchen and make it comfortable for yourself. a pressure cooker is a unique miracle machine that has many talents. Imagine that now you don't need to buy a slow cooker, pressure cooker, rice cooker, steamer, yogurt machine, or any other useful pots - all these functions already exist in this multitalented device.

The utility of the appliance also means that using the Ninja Foodi, you will be able to craft all of your dishes from mains, desserts to yogurt and even baked goods!
The Ninja Foodi Multi-Crisp Cooker is nothing short of a revolutionary cooking appliance that has seemingly taken the whole culinary world by storm!
Developed by a team of food industry experts and produced by one of the world's most well-known food technology firms, the Ninja Foodi Multi-Crisp Cooker has received numerous awards in it's brief little existence! Of course, these are secondary accolades to the prize of greater culinary adoration offered by this cooking appliance!
As one of the first cooking appliances to be sold on the consumer market that has actually been designed and built to cook. And not just heat! In fact, the Ninja Foodi Multi-Crisp Cooker offers next-level precision, versatility and ingredients haven't been seen in any kitchen up to this point! Helping you to cook food exactly the way you want it!
You know those nice, crispy, golden brown chicken nuggets you get from the fast food joint down the street? You can make those with the Ninja Foodi Multi-Crisp Cooker! No, you're not limited to just deep frying dishes with this appliance either. The Ninja Foodi Multi-Crisp Cooker can also deep fry vegetables and recipe-ready meals!
This is the 21st Century, where dieting has become a big deal in the modern world and a lot of restaurants are getting on board with the idea of incorporating healthier ingredient options into their menu. Especially for kids eat.
To get the perfect food, it's very important to keep the pressure cooker clean. Wash the kitchen tool thoroughly after each use. Cleaning the pressure cooker does not take much time and effort. To do this, you need a cloth or fabric and a dishwasher and vinegar. The heat that the dishwasher gets rid of any fat residue in the pot while vinegar eliminates the smell that remains after cooking.
It is worth remembering that you need to wash only the removable parts of the device. Also, you should unplug the pressure cooker before extracting parts from the gadget.
Make sure that all the washed parts of the pressure cooker are completely dry before placing them back into the pressure cooker. Another easy way to clean the pressure cooker by hand is to combine the vinegar, water, and 1 tablespoon of lemon juice in the pressure cooker and set the program to "Steam. " This method will clean the pot without using a dishwasher or doing so by hand and help you to avoid the smell after cooking pressure cooker.

You will get easy to make recipes, meat, poultry, seafood, the list goes on!
And if you are daring and want to take on more of a challenge, then a good number of slightly complicated recipes are also there to challenge your inner chef!
All of these recipes are carefully chosen to help you lose weight in the long run and become a "Better" version of yourself!

BREAKFAST

BREAKFAST

Coconut Oatmeal

PREPARATION TIME 25 MINUTES
COOKING TIME 18 MINUTES
SERVINGS 6 PERSONS

Ingredients:

- 85 grams shredded dried coconut flakes
- 675 ml coconut milk
- 750 ml water
- 36.7 g psyllium husks
- 61.5 g coconut flour
- 312 g vanilla extract
- 1.32 g cinnamon
- 97.5 g granulated stevia

Instructions:

- Add all of the ingredients into the Ninja Foodi and stir together briefly
- Place the lid on and set the steamer valve to seal. Set the pressure cooker function to 1 minute (it will take about 10 minutes to come to pressure).
- When the oatmeal is done, do a quick pressure release by opening the steamer valve carefully. Serve while hot

CALORIES: 202KCAL | FAT: 16G | CARBOHYDRATE: 6G | PROTEIN: 3G

BREAKFAST

Almond Spice Oatmeal

PREPARATION TIME
15 MINUTES

COOKING TIME
20 MINUTES

SERVINGS
6 PERSONS

Ingredients:

- 105 g chopped almonds
- 720 ml almond milk
- 500 ml water
- 73.5 g psyllium husks
- 7.5 g vanilla extract
- 1.32 g cinnamon
- 0.59 g nutmeg
- 96 g granulated stevia

Instructions:

- Add all of the ingredients into the Ninja Foodi and stir together briefly
- Place the lid on and set the steamer valve to seal.
- Set the pressure cooker function to 1 minute (it will take about 10 minutes to come to pressure).
- When the oatmeal is done, do a quick pressure release by opening the steamer valve carefully.
- Serve while hot

CALORIES: 136KCAL | FAT: 9G | CARBOHYDRATE:3G | PROTEIN: 4G

BREAKFAST

Carrot Cake Oats

PREPARATION TIME: 10 MINUTES
COOKING TIME: 13 MINUTES
SERVINGS: 8 PERSONS

Ingredients:

- 312 g oats
- 250 g water
- 960 ml unsweetened vanilla almond milk
- 2 apples, diced
- 180 g shredded carrot
- 130 g dried cranberries
- 118 ml maple syrup
- 5.28 g cinnamon
- 5.28 g vanilla extract

Instructions:

- Place all the ingredients in the pot. Assemble pressure lid, making sure the pressure release valve is in the seal position.
- Select pressure and set time to 3 minutes. Select start/stop to begin.
- When pressure cooking is complete, allow pressure to naturally release for 10 minutes. Then quick release remaining pressure by moving the pressure release valve to the vent position. Carefully remove lid when unit has finished releasing pressure.
- Stir oats, allowing them to cool, and serve with toppings such as chopped walnuts, diced pineapple, or shredded coconut, if desired.

CALORIES: 252KCAL | FAT: 3G | CARBOHYDRATE: 54G | PROTEIN: 4G

BREAKFAST

Morning Casserole

PREPARATION TIME 15 MINUTES | **COOKING TIME** 45 MINUTES | **SERVINGS** 3 PERSONS

Ingredients:

- 99 g cauliflower hash brown, cooked
- 3 eggs, whisked
- 177 ml almond milk
- 56.70 of g chorizo, chopped
- 28 g mozzarella, sliced
- 35 g chili flakes
- 2.4 g butter

Instructions:

- Melt the butter and whisk it together with the chili flakes, chorizo, almond milk, and eggs.
- Add hash brown and stir gently.
- Place the egg mixture in the cake pan and place in the Ninja Foodi.
- Cook on Air Crisp 185°C for 8 minutes.
- Then add sliced mozzarella on the top and cook for 2 minutes more, or until you get the desired doneness.
- Enjoy!

CALORIES: 326KCAL | FAT: 28.2G | CARBOHYDRATE: 5.8G | PROTEIN: 14.2G

BREAKFAST

Butter Chicken Bites

PREPARATION TIME 22 MINUTES
COOKING TIME 18 MINUTES
SERVINGS 3 PERSONS

Ingredients:

- 284 g chicken thighs, boneless, skinless
- 3.18g turmeric
- 2.71 g chili flakes
- 6.00 g salt
- 0.59 g ground nutmeg
- 1.32 g ground ginger
- 240 g Double cream
- 28.35 g butters
- 6.00 g kosher salt

Instructions:

- Preheat Ninja Foodi pot at Sauté/Stir mode for 5 minutes.
- Toss the butter in the pot and melt it.
- Add turmeric, chili flakes, salt, and ground nutmeg. Then, add ground ginger and salt. Bring to boil the mixture.
- Meanwhile, chop the chicken thighs roughly.
- Transfer the chicken thighs in the pot and cooks for 5 minutes at Sauté mode.
- After this, add heavy cream and close the lid. Seal the lid. Select Pressure mode and set High pressure
- Cook it for 6 minutes. Then make a quick pressure release.
- Chill the cooked chicken bites little and serve!

CALORIES: 322KCAL | FAT: 22.3G | CARBOHYDRATE: 1.5G | PROTEIN: 28G

BREAKFAST

Bangers & Mash

PREPARATION TIME: 10 MINUTES
COOKING TIME: 45 MINUTES
SERVINGS: 6 PERSONS

Ingredients:

FOR THE BANGERS:
- 6 bratwurst sausages (or your preferred sausage)
- 475ml beef stock, divided
- 2 large sweet onions, cut into half-inch slices
- 28 g olive oil
- 15 g corn flour
- 6.00 g fine sea salt
- 3.50 g black pepper
- 0.23 g thyme

FOR THE MASH:
- 590ml water
- 900g Yukon gold and russet potatoes, peeled and diced
- 86g butter
- 44 g single cream

FOR THE PEAS:
- 385g frozen peas
- 14.17 g butter
- Salt and pepper, to taste

Instructions:

- Add 2 tbsp. olive oil to the inner pot of your Ninja Foodi and select the SEAR/SAUTÉ function. Add the sausages and cook on high until browned, flipping them as necessary. Add the onions and sauté for 5 to 10 minutes or until they begin to brown.
- Place the pressure-cooking lid on the multi-cooker, making sure that the nozzle is in the VENT position. Adjust the heat to medium and cook for 10 minutes or until the sausages' internal temperature reaches 71 to 84°C.
- Mix 1 to 2 tbsp. beef stock with the corn flour to make it slurry; set aside.
- Take the pressure lid off and deglaze the pot with the beef stock, scraping the bottom with a wooden or silicone spatula to remove any remaining browned bits.
- Stir in the thyme, salt and black pepper.
- Stir in the corn-starch slurry and continue to cook on medium in SEAR/SAUTÉ mode for approximately 5 minutes or until the sauce thickens.
- Turn the Ninja Foodi off, transfer the sausages into an 8x2inch round cake pan, and pour the gravy over the sausages. Wash the inner pot of the Ninja Foodi and return it to the unit.
- Place the diffuser for the Cook & Crisp basket in the bottom of the pot, making sure that the pointed legs are pointing upwards.
- Add 590ml of water and add the potatoes to the pot. Remember to place them in the open areas between the diffuser legs to help the pan fit in the centre.
- Cover the pan with a silicone cover and place it on the diffuser.
- Place the peas in a 6x2inch round pan and cover it with foil (or a silicone cover). Place the pan on top of the 8x2inch covered pan.
- Put the cooking pressure lid on the Ninja Foodi and move the nozzle to the seal position.
- Select PRESSURE and cook on high for 10 minutes. When the timer beeps, use the quick release to lower the pressure.
- Carefully remove the pan containing the peas from the unit. Remove the cover, add the butter to the peas and season with salt. Cover the pan again and it set aside until you're ready to serve.
- Carefully tip the cover of the 8x2inch pan to remove the accumulated liquid on top of it. Then, carefully remove the pan from the unit and set it aside.
- Remove the diffuser from the unit and scoop the potatoes out into a large mixing bowl.
- Mash the potatoes slightly with a hand mixer (turned off) to let the steam escape. Add the butter, salt, and cream (or half and half), then

CALORIES 724; PROTEIN 27G; CARBOHYDRATES 37G; FAT 52G; FIBRE 8G; SODIUM 1413MG; SUGAR 6G

BREAKFAST

Breakfast Broccoli Casserole

PREPARATION TIME
17 MINUTES

COOKING TIME
22 MINUTES

SERVINGS
4 PERSONS

Ingredients:

- 13.7 g extra-virgin olive oil
- 453.6g broccoli, cut into florets
- 450 g cauliflower, cut into florets
- 24 g almond flour
- 456 g coconut milk
- 1.19 g ground nutmeg
- Pinch of pepper
- 168 g shredded Gouda

Instructions:

- Pre-heat your Ninja Foodi by setting it to Sauté mode
- Add olive oil and let it heat up, add broccoli and cauliflower
- Take a medium bowl stir in almond flour, coconut milk, nutmeg, pepper, 1 cup cheese and add the mixture to your Ninja Foodi
- Top with ½ cup cheese and lock lid, cook on high pressure for 5 minutes
- Release pressure naturally over 10 minutes
- Serve and enjoy!

CALORIES 373, PROTEIN 16G CARBOHYDRATES 6G, FAT 32G.

BREAKFAST

Creamy Asparagus Soup

PREPARATION TIME 20 MINUTES | **COOKING TIME** 20 MINUTES | **SERVINGS** 4 PERSONS

Ingredients:

- 13.3 g olive oil
- 3 green onions, sliced crosswise into 0.006 pieces
- 454 g asparagus
- 950 ml vegetable stock
- 14.2g unsalted butter
- 6 g almond flour
- 11 g salts
- 7.20 g white pepper
- 120 g Double cream

Instructions:

- Set your Ninja Foodi to "Sauté" mode and add oil, let it heat up
- Add green onions and Sauté for a few minutes, add asparagus and stock
- Lock lid and cook on high pressure for 5 minutes
- Take a small saucepan and place it over low heat, add butter, flour and stir until the mixture foams and turns into a golden beige, this is your blond roux
- Remove from heat and release pressure naturally over 10 minutes
- Open lid and add roux, salt and pepper to the soup
- Use an immersion blender to puree the soup
- Taste and season accordingly, swirl in cream and enjoy!

CALORIES 192, PROTEIN 6G CARBOHYDRATES 8G FAT 14G.

BREAKFAST

Potato and Chorizo Frittata

PREPARATION TIME 10 MINUTES
COOKING TIME 20 MINUTES
SERVINGS 4 PERSONS

Ingredients:

- 4 eggs
- 250 ml milk
- Sea salt as required
- Freshly ground black pepper as required
- 1 potato, diced
- 25 g frozen corn
- 1 chorizo sausage, diced
- 225 g feta cheese, crumbled
- 250 ml water

Instructions:

- In a medium bowl, whisk together the eggs and milk. Season with salt and pepper.
- Place the potato, corn, and chorizo in the Multi-Purpose Pan or an 8-inch baking pan. Pour the egg mixture and feta cheese over top. Cover the pan with aluminium foil and place on the Reversible Rack. Make sure it's in the lower position.
- Pour the water into the pot. Assemble pressure lid, making sure the pressure release valve is in the seal position.
- Select pressure and set to HI. Set time to 20 minutes. Select start/stop to begin
- When pressure cooking is complete, quick release the pressure by moving the pressure release valve to the vent position. Carefully remove lid when unit has finished releasing pressure.
- Remove the pan from pot and place it on a cooling rack for 5 minutes, then serve.

CALORIES: 361; PROTEIN: 21G; CARBOHYDRATES: 17G; FAT: 24G; FIBER: 2G; SODIUM: 972MG.

BREAKFAST

Curried Chickpea and Roasted Tomato

PREPARATION TIME
10 MINUTES

COOKING TIME
30 MINUTES

SERVINGS
6 PERSONS

Ingredients:

- 26.6 g extra-virgin olive oil
- 2 red bell peppers, diced
- 1 small onion, diced
- 2 garlic cloves, minced
- 26.6 g red curry paste
- 14.1 g tomato paste
- 1 can crushed fire-roasted tomatoes
- 1 can chickpeas, rinsed and drained
- Kosher salt to taste
- Freshly ground black pepper as required
- 6 large eggs
- 16 g chopped coriander

Instructions:

- Select sear/sauté and set to high. Select start/stop to begin. Add the olive oil and let preheat for 5 minutes.
- Add the bell peppers, onion, and garlic and cook for 3 minutes, stirring occasionally.
- Add the curry and tomato pastes and cook for 2 minutes, stirring occasionally.
- Add the crushed tomatoes, chickpeas, and season with salt and pepper and stir. Assemble pressure lid, making sure the pressure release valve is in the seal position.
- Select pressure and set to high. Set time to 10 minutes. Select start/stop to begin.
- When pressure cooking is complete, quick release the pressure by turning the pressure release valve to the vent position. Carefully remove the lid when the unit has finished releasing pressure.
- With the back of a spoon, make six indents in the sauce. Crack an egg into each indent. Close crisping lid.
- Select bake/roast, set temperature to 177ºC, and set time to 10 minutes (or until eggs are cooked to your liking). Select start/stop to begin.
- When cooking is complete, open lid. Let cool 5 to 10 minutes, then garnish with the cilantro and serve. If desired, serve with crusty bread, chopped scallions, feta cheese, and/or pickled jalapeños.

CALORIES: 258; PROTEIN: 11G CARBOHYDRATES: 27G; FAT: 12G; FIBRE: 6G; SODIUM: 444MG.

BREAKFAST

Buttered Up Garlic and Fennel

PREPARATION TIME
10 MINUTES

COOKING TIME
2.5 MINUTES

SERVINGS
4 PERSONS

Ingredients:

- 680 g fennel bulbs, cut into wedges
- 1.55 g dried dill weed
- 14.8 g dry white wine
- ½ stick butter
- 2 garlic cloves, sliced
- 0.90 g cayenne
- 550 ml stock
- 3 g salt
- 0.58 g ground black

Instructions:

- Set your Ninja Foodi on "Sauté" mode
- Then add butter, let it heat up
- Add garlic and cook for 30 seconds
- Add rest of the ingredients
- Close the lid and cook on low pressure for 2 minutes
- Remove the lid once done
- Serve and enjoy!

CALORIES: 121KCAL PROTEIN: 2G CARBOHYDRATES: 1G FAT: 12G FIBRE: 1G SODIUM: 537MG SUGAR: 1G

BREAKFAST

Broccoli and Scrambled Cheese Breakfast

PREPARATION TIME 15 MINUTES
COOKING TIME 20 MINUTES
SERVINGS 4 PERSONS

Ingredients:

- 1 pack, 106 g frozen broccoli florets
- 28.35 g butter
- salt to taste
- pepper as needed
- 8 whole eggs
- 30 ml milk
- 169 g white cheddar cheese, shredded
- Crushed red pepper, as needed

Instructions:

- Add butter and broccoli to your Ninja Foodi
- Season with salt and pepper according to your taste
- Set the Ninja to Medium Pressure mode and let it cook for about 10 minutes, covered, making sure to keep stirring the broccoli from time to time
- Take a medium sized bowl and add crack in the eggs, beat the eggs gently
- Pour milk into the eggs and give it a nice stir
- Add the egg mixture into the Ninja (over broccoli) and gently stir, cook for 2 minutes (uncovered)
- Once the egg has settled in, add cheese and sprinkle red pepper, black pepper, and salt
- Enjoy with bacon strips if you prefer!

CALORIES 197, FAT 13G, CARBOHYDRATES 5G, PROTEIN 14G

BREAKFAST

Asparagus Frittata

PREPARATION TIME
10 MINUTES

COOKING TIME
15 MINUTES

SERVINGS
2 PERSONS

Ingredients:

- 56.7 g asparagus, chopped
- 3 eggs, whisked
- 30 ml almond milk
- 2.00 g almond flour
- 3 g salt
- 0.45 g cayenne pepper
- 5.62 g Parmesan, grated
- 5 ml coconut oil

Instructions:

- Preheat the pot on "Sauté mode.
- Add coconut oil and chopped asparagus.
- Sauté the vegetable for 3 minutes.
- Meanwhile, mix up together the almond milk, whisked, eggs, almond flour, cayenne pepper, and grated cheese.
- Pour the egg mixture into the pot.
- Close the lid and seal it. Cook the frittata on High (Pressure mode) for 15 minutes.
- After this, make a quick pressure release.
- Lower the air fryer lid and cook the meal at 204ºC for 6 minutes more.
- When the surface of the frittata is crusty enough – finish cooking and serve it!

CALORIES 165, PROTEIN 11.8G CARBOHYDRATES 3.1G FAT 12.3G,

BREAKFAST

Breakfast Muffins

PREPARATION TIME 25 MINUTES | **COOKING TIME** 15 MINUTES | **SERVINGS** 2 PERSONS

Ingredients:

- 4.7g butter
- 15 g cream cheese
- 6.00 g almond flour
- 1 egg, beaten
- 59 g Cheddar, grated
- 3 g salt
- 1.42 g black pepper
- 125 ml water (for cooking on High)

Instructions:

- Mix up together the cream cheese, butter, egg, cheese, almond flour, ground black pepper, paprika and salt.
- Whisk the mixture until smooth. Afterwards, pour ½ cup water in the pot. Insert the rack.
- Transfer the batter in the prepared muffins moulds and place on the rack
- Cover the muffins with the foil and close the lid.
- Make sure you seal the lid and cook on Pressure mode (High) for 15 minutes
- Then make the quick pressure release for 5 minutes
- Chill the muffins little and serve

CALORIES 203, FAT 17G, CARBOHYDRATES 1.9G, PROTEIN 11.1G

BREAKFAST

Curry Shredded Chicken

PREPARATION TIME
45 MINUTES

COOKING TIME
15 MINUTES

SERVINGS
2 PERSONS

Ingredients:

- 454 g chicken breast, skinless, boneless
- 5.33 g curry paste
- 28.35 g butter
- 1.77 g cayenne pepper
- 125 ml of water

Instructions:

- Rub the chicken breast with the curry paste and place in the pot.
- Sprinkle the poultry with cayenne pepper and add butter.
- Pour water in the pot and close the lid. Seal the lid.
- Set Pressure mode and cook on High for 30 minutes.
- Then make natural pressure release for 10 minutes.
- Open the lid and shred the chicken inside the pot with the help of the fork.
- Then close the lid and sauté the chicken for 5 minutes more. Serve it!

CALORIES 380, FAT 18.8G, CARBOHYDRATES 1.2G, PROTEIN 48.4G

BREAKFAST

Mashed Cauliflower Delight

PREPARATION TIME 10 MINUTES **COOKING TIME** 5 MINUTES **SERVINGS** 4 PERSONS

Ingredients:

- 1 large head cauliflower, chopped into large pieces
- 1 garlic clove, minced
- 13.8 g ghee
- 70 g cashew cream
- 2.02 g fresh chives, minced
- Salt and pepper to taste

Instructions:

- Add the pot to your Ninja Foodi and add water
- Add steamer basket on top and add cauliflower pieces
- Close the lid and cook for 5 minutes on "High"
- Quick-release the pressure
- Now add the remaining ingredients
- Open the lid and use your blender to mash the cauliflower
- Blend until you get a smooth mixture. Serve and enjoy!

CALORIES: 59KCAL PROTEIN: 1G CARBOHYDRATES: 2G FAT: 5G SODIUM: 61MG

BREAKFAST

Great Brussels Bite

PREPARATION TIME
5 MINUTES

COOKING TIME
3 MINUTES

SERVINGS
4 PERSONS

Ingredients:

- 15 medium Brussels sprouts
- 33.75g pine nuts
- Salt to taste
- Pepper as required
- Olive oil as needed
- 240ml water l

Instructions:

- Place a steamer basket in your Ninja Foodi and add Brussels to the basket
- Add water and lock lid, cook on high pressure for 3 minutes
- Quick release pressure
- Transfer Brussels to a plate and toss with olive oil, salt, pepper and sprinkle of pine nuts
- Enjoy!

CALORIES: 112 PROTEIN: 5G CARBOHYDRATES: 4G FAT: 7G

POULTRY RECIPES

CHICKEN AND POULTRY

Chicken Bean Bake

PREPARATION TIME 8 MINUTES

COOKING TIME 17 MINUTES

SERVINGS 8 PERSONS

Ingredients:

- ½ red onion, diced
- ½ red bell pepper, diced
- 1 tablespoon extra-virgin olive oil
- 225g boneless, skinless chicken breasts cut into 1-inch cubes
- 202 g white rice
- 425g corn, rinsed
- 285g roasted tomatoes with chiles
- 425g black beans, rinsed and drained
- 30g packet taco seasoning
- 166 g shredded Cheddar cheese
- 475 ml chicken broth
- Kosher salt as required
- Ground Black pepper to taste

Instructions:

- Put in the chicken and mix for about 2-3 minutes to brown evenly.
- Add the onion and bell pepper, stir-cook until softened for 2 minutes. Add the rice, tomatoes, beans, corn, taco seasoning, broth, salt, and pepper, combine well.
- Seal the multi-cooker by locking it with the pressure lid; ensure to keep the pressure release valve locked/sealed.
- Select "Pressure" mode and select the "High" pressure level. Then after, set the timer to 7 minutes and press "Start/Stop," it will start the cooking process by building up inside pressure.
- When the timer goes off, quickly release pressure by adjusting the pressure valve to "Vent", after pressure gets released, open the pressure lid. Add the cheese on top.
- Seal the multi-cooker by locking it with the Crisping Lid; ensure to keep the pressure release valve locked/sealed.
- Select "Broil" mode and select the "High" pressure level. Then after, set the timer to 8 minutes and press "Start/Stop" it will start the cooking process by building up inside pressure.

307 CALORIES; PROTEIN 36G; CARBOHYDRATES 30G; FAT 4.9G; FIBRE 9.5G; SODIUM 759MG

CHICKEN AND POULTRY

Shredded Salsa Chicken

PREPARATION TIME
5 MINUTES

COOKING TIME
20 MINUTES

SERVINGS
4 PERSONS

Ingredients:

- 450g chicken breast, skin and bones removed
- 275 g chunky salsa Keto friendly
- 3 g salt
- Pinch of oregano
- 1.52 g cumin
- Pepper to taste

Instructions:

- Season chicken with all the listed spices, then add to Ninja Foodi
- Cover with salsa and close the lid
- Cook on "High" pressure for 20 minutes
- Quick-release the pressure
- Add chicken to a platter then shred the chicken
- Serve and enjoy!

CALORIES: 235KCAL PROTEIN: 23G CARBOHYDRATES: 3G FAT: 14G

CHICKEN AND POULTRY

Barbecue Chicken

PREPARATION TIME 4 MINUTES

COOKING TIME 10 MINUTES

SERVINGS 4 PERSONS

Ingredients:

- 13.3 g olive oil
- 3 chicken breasts (boneless and skinless)
- 1 teaspoon garlic powder
- Salt and pepper to taste
- 225 g barbecue sauce
- 125 g water

Instructions:

- Pour the olive oil into the Ninja Foodi. Add the rest of the ingredients. Mix well.
- Pour the barbecue sauce over the chicken. Do not stir. Seal the pot.
- Set it to pressure. Cook at "High" pressure for 10 minutes.
- Release the pressure naturally. Shred the chicken meat and toss in barbecue sauce.
- Serve with steamed vegetables.

CALORIES 352 PROTEIN 27G CARBOHYDRATES 7G FAT 24G FIBRE 1G SODIUM 616MG SUGAR 4G

CHICKEN AND POULTRY

Chicken Chile Verde

PREPARATION TIME 7 MINUTES

COOKING TIME 25 MINUTES

SERVINGS 4 PERSONS

Ingredients:

- 900g chicken thighs
- 1/4 teaspoon garlic powder
- 450g salsa Verde
- 1.01g ground cumin
- Salt to taste
- Pepper as required

Instructions:

- Add the chicken to the Ninja Foodi.
- Season with the garlic powder, salsa verde, and cumin. Cover the pot.
- Set it to "Pressure". Cook at "High" pressure for 25 minutes.
- Release the pressure quickly. Shred the chicken using 2 forks.
- Season with the salt and pepper.
- Serve with whole wheat tortillas.

CALORIES: 241KCAL PROTEIN: 29G CARBOHYDRATES: 9G FAT: 10G FIBRE: 2G SODIUM: 1003MG SUGAR: 5G

CHICKEN AND POULTRY

Lemon and Chicken Extravaganza

PREPARATION TIME
5 MINUTES

COOKING TIME
24 MINUTES

SERVINGS
4 PERSONS

Ingredients:

- 4 bone-in, skin-on chicken thighs
- Salt to taste
- Pepper as required
- 28.35 g butter, divided
- 6.56 g garlic, minced
- 100 ml herbed chicken stock
- 120 g Double cream
- 1/2 a lemon, juiced

Instructions:

- Season your chicken thighs generously with salt and pepper
- Set your Foodi to "Sauté" mode and add oil, let it heat up
- Add thigh, Sauté both sides for 6 minutes. Remove thigh to a platter and keep it on the side
- Add garlic, cook for 2 minutes. Whisk in chicken stock, double cream, lemon juice and gently stir
- Bring the mix to a simmer and reintroduce chicken
- Lock lid and cook for 10 minutes on "High" pressure
- Release pressure over 10 minutes. Serve and enjoy!

CALORIES 560 PROTEIN 46G CARBOHYDRATES 9G FAT 38G FIBER 1G SODIUM 1109MG SUGAR 1G

CHICKEN AND POULTRY

Lemon Chicken with Garlic

PREPARATION TIME 5 MINUTES
COOKING TIME 14 MINUTES
SERVINGS 4 PERSONS

Ingredients:

- 6 chicken thighs
- Salt to taste
- pepper as required
- 1.35 g red chili flakes
- 1.64 g garlic powder
- 1.15 g smoked paprika
- 26.6 g olive oil
- 44.36 ml butter
- 1 onion, chopped
- 4 cloves garlic, minced
- 14.4 g lemon juice
- 60 g low sodium stock
- 0.3 g Italian seasoning
- Lemon zest
- 30 ml double cream

Instructions:

- Sprinkle the chicken thighs with salt, pepper, chili flakes, garlic powder, and paprika.
- Set the Ninja Foodi to "Sauté". Add the olive oil.
- Cook the chicken for 3 minutes per side. Remove from the pot and set aside.
- Melt the butter in the pot. Add the onion and garlic. Deglaze the pot with the lemon juice. Cook for 1 minute. Add the chicken broth, seasoning, and lemon zest.
- Set the pot to "Pressure". Seal it. Cook at high pressure for 7 minutes.
- Release the pressure naturally. Stir in the heavy cream before serving.

CALORIES 430 PROTEIN 31G CARBOHYDRATES 9G FAT 41G FIBER 1G SODIUM 164MG SUGAR 6G

CHICKEN AND POULTRY

Chicken Cacciatore

PREPARATION TIME
4 MINUTES

COOKING TIME
32 MINUTES

SERVINGS
4 PERSONS

Ingredients:

- 4 chicken thighs
- 30 ml olive oil
- 1/2 onion, chopped
- 2 cloves garlic, minced
- 3 stalks celery, chopped
- 115g mushrooms
- 400g stewed tomatoes
- 1.6g herb de Provence
- 177 ml water
- 3 cubes chicken bouillon, crumbled
- 2 tablespoons tomato paste

Instructions:

- Set the Ninja Foodi to "Sauté". Add the oil and chicken.
- Cook the chicken for 6 minutes per side. Remove the chicken and set aside.
- Add the onion, garlic, celery, and mushrooms. Cook for 5 minutes, stirring frequently.
- Put the chicken back. Pour in the tomatoes and tomato paste.
- Add the rest of the ingredients. Seal the pot.
- Set it to "Pressure". Cook at "High" pressure for 15 minutes. Release the pressure quickly.
- Serve with pasta or rice.

CALORIES: 310KCAL PROTEIN: 27G CARBOHYDRATES: 22G FAT: FIBRE: 5G SODIUM: 511MG SUGAR: 11G.

CHICKEN AND POULTRY

Turkey Bean Chili

PREPARATION TIME 12 MINUTES

COOKING TIME 30 MINUTES

SERVINGS 6 PERSONS

Ingredients:

- 2 garlic cloves, minced
- 680g turkey, ground
- 15 ml extra-virgin olive oil
- 1 onion, chopped
- 3g oregano, dried
- 6.09 g ground cumin
- 425g of beans, rinsed and drained
- 0.74 g sea salt
- 0.4 g black pepper, freshly ground
- 950 ml chicken stock
- 1 pack biscuits

Instructions:

- In the pot, add the oil; Select "Sear/Sauté" mode and select "MD: HI" pressure level.
- Press "Start/Stop." After about 4-5 minutes, the oil will start simmering.
- Add the onions, garlic, and cook (while stirring) for 2-3 minutes until they become softened and translucent.
- Add the turkey, cumin, oregano, beans, broth, salt, and black pepper; stir the mixture.
- Seal the multi-cooker by locking it with the pressure lid; ensure to keep the pressure release valve locked/sealed.
- Select "Pressure" mode and select the "HI" pressure level. Then, set the timer to 10 minutes and press "Start/Stop"; it will start the cooking process by building up inside pressure.
- At the point when the clock goes off, speedy discharge pressure by adjusting the pressure valve to the "Vent". After pressure gets released, open the pressure lid.
- Arrange the biscuits in a single layer over the mixture.
- Seal the multi-cooker by locking it with the crisping lid; ensure to keep the pressure release valve locked/sealed. Select "Broil" mode and select the "HI" pressure level.
- Then, set the timer to 15 minutes and press " Start/Stop"; it will start the cooking process by building up inside pressure.
- At the point when the clock goes off, speedy discharge pressure by adjusting the pressure valve to the "Vent".

CALORIES 211; PROTEIN 22.5G; CARBOHYDRATES 16.4G; FAT 6.5G; FIBRE 4.7G; SODIUM 474MG

CHICKEN AND POULTRY

Honey Teriyaki Chicken

PREPARATION TIME
6 MINUTES

COOKING TIME
30 MINUTES

SERVINGS
4 PERSONS

Ingredients:

- 4 chicken breasts, sliced into strips
- 255 g of soy sauce
- 125 ml water
- 226.7g honey
- 5.6 g garlic, minced
- 277.5 g rice vinegar
- 0.88 g ground ginger
- 0.5 g crushed red pepper flakes
- 24.36 g corn-starch dissolved in 44.36 ml cold water

Instructions:

- Put the chicken inside the Ninja Foodi.
- Add the rest of the ingredients except the corn starch mixture.
- Put on the lid. Set it to pressure, cook at "High" pressure for 30 minutes.
- Release the pressure naturally. Set it to "Sauté".
- Stir in the corn-starch and simmer until the sauce has thickened.
- Garnish with sesame seeds and serve with fried rice.

CALORIES: 350 KCAL, PROTEIN: 31 G, CARBOHYDRATES: 51 G, FAT: 4 G
FIBRE: 1 G, SUGAR SODIUM: 3378 MG, 47 G

CHICKEN AND POULTRY

Chicken Balls in Melted Butter

PREPARATION TIME 40 MINUTES

COOKING TIME 20 MINUTES

SERVINGS 8 PERSONS

Ingredients:

- 420 g ground chicken
- 4 tablespoons butter
- 26 g dill
- 6g salt
- 2.30 g paprika
- 2.33 g ground black pepper
- 3.28 g garlic powder
- 5 ml olive oil
- 1 egg
- 48 g pork rinds

Instructions:

- Chop the dill and put the chopped dill in the mixing bowl.
- Add salt, paprika, ground black pepper, garlic powder, and ground chicken. Stir the mixture using a wooden spoon.
- Add egg and blend well using your hands. Make medium-sized balls from the ground chicken mixture. Flatten them well and put a pat of butter in the middle of every ball.
- Wrap the ground chicken around the butter to make the chicken balls. Dip the chicken balls in the pork rinds. Pour the olive oil in the pressure cooker and add the chicken balls.
- Close the lid and cook the dish on" Sauté" mode for 25 minutes. When the cooking time ends, open the pressure cooker lid and transfer the chicken balls to serving plates.

CALORIES: 226, FAT: 14.1G, CARBOHYDRATES: 2.8G, PROTEIN: 22.4G

CHICKEN AND POULTRY

Summer Time Chicken Salad

PREPARATION TIME
10 MINUTES

COOKING TIME
10 MINUTES

SERVINGS
4 PERSONS

Ingredients:

- 8 boneless chicken thighs
- Kosher salt as required
- 12.19g of ghee
- 1 small onion, chopped
- 2 medium carrots, chopped
- ½ a pound of cremini mushrooms
- 3 garlic cloves, peeled and crushed
- 400 g cherry tomatoes
- 90 g pitted green olives
- 28 g freshly cracked black pepper
- 10.05g of thinly sliced basil leaves
- 15 g of coarsely chopped parsley

Instructions:

- Season the chicken thigh with ¾ teaspoon of kosher salt and keep it in your fridge for about 2 days
- Set your Ninja Foodi to Sauté mode and add ghee and allow it to melt
- Once the Ghee is simmering, add carrots, onions, mushrooms and ½ a teaspoon of salt
- Sauté the veggies until they are tender (should be around 3-5 minutes)
- Drop the tomato paste and garlic to your pot and cook for 30 seconds
- Add seasoned chicken to the pot alongside olives and cherry tomatoes
- Give everything a stir
- Lock up the lid and cook for 7-10 minutes at HIGH pressure
- Once done, allow the pressure to quick release
- Stir in fresh herbs and enjoy!

CHICKEN AND POULTRY

The Great Poblano Chicken Curry

PREPARATION TIME 10 MINUTES
COOKING TIME 15 MINUTES
SERVINGS 4 PERSONS

Ingredients:

- 115 g onion, diced
- 3 poblano peppers, chopped
- 5 garlic cloves,
- 64 g diced
- 680g large chicken breast chunks
- 4g cilantro, chopped
- 1.69 g ground coriander
- 2 g ground cumin
- 11.38 g salt
- 591ml of water
- 59.6ml cream cheese

Instructions:

- Add everything to your Ninja Foodi except cheese and lock up the lid
- Cook on high pressure for 15 minutes. Release the pressure naturally over 10 minutes
- Remove the chicken with tongs and place it on the side
- Use an immersion blender to blend the soup and veggies. Set your pot to Sauté mode
- Once the stock is hot, add cream cheese (Cut in chunks). Whisk well
- Shred the chicken and transfer it back to the pot. Serve and enjoy!

CALORIES 375.4 PROTEIN 35.5 G CARBOHYDRATE 25.8 G FAT 15.2 G FIBRE 5.5 G SODIUM 742.7 MG SUGARS 4.3 G

CHICKEN AND POULTRY

Chili Chicken Wings

PREPARATION TIME
40 MINUTES

COOKING TIME
17 MINUTES

SERVINGS
4 PERSONS

Ingredients:

- 120 ml hot sauce
- 118g water
- 28.35 g butter
- 14.4 g apple cider vinegar
- 923g frozen chicken wings
- 1.15 g paprika

Instructions:

- Add all the ingredients into the cook and crisp basket and place the basket inside the Ninja Foodi
- Place the pressure cooker lid on top of the pot and close the pressure valve to the seal position. Set the pressure cooker function to high heat and set the timer for 5 minutes
- Once the cooking cycle is complete, release the pressure quickly by carefully opening the steamer valve
- Serve hot

CALORIES 311, FAT 23G, CARBOHYDRATES 0G, PROTEIN 24G

CHICKEN AND POULTRY

Cajun Turkey Breast

PREPARATION TIME 5 MINUTES
COOKING TIME 35 MINUTES
SERVINGS 8 PERSONS

Ingredients:

- ½ red onion, diced
- 1 (1,814g) boneless, skinless turkey breast
- 36g Cajun spice seasoning
- 18.00 g kosher salt
- 118 ml water

Instructions:

- Season turkey breast liberally, evenly, and on all sides with the Cajun spice seasoning and salt.
- Pour the water into the pot. Place the Cook & Crisp Basket in the pot, then place the turkey into the basket. Assemble pressure lid, making sure the pressure release valve is in the seal position.
- Select pressure and set to HI. Set time to 20 minutes. Select start/stop to begin.
- When pressure cooking is complete, quick release the pressure by moving the pressure release valve to the vent position. Carefully remove lid when unit has finished releasing pressure.
- Close crisping lid. Select air crisp, set temperature to 182.04 Celsius and set time to 15 minutes. Select start/stop to begin.
- When cooking is complete, open lid and transfer the turkey breast to a cutting board. Let rest for at least 10 minutes before slicing or serving.

CALORIES: 229; PROTEIN: 54G CARBOHYDRATES: 0G; FAT: 1G; FIBER: 0G; SODIUM: 230MG;

CHICKEN AND POULTRY

Hearty Chicken Yum

PREPARATION TIME
30 MINUTES

COOKING TIME
40 MINUTES

SERVINGS
4 PERSONS

Ingredients:

- 270g fresh boneless chicken thigh
- 44.7g ketchup
- 8.9g salt
- 6.56 g garlic powder
- 55.17g ghee
- 1.2g ground black pepper
- 54g organic tamari
- 48g stevia

Instructions:

- Add the listed ingredients to your Ninja Foodi and give it a nice stir
- Lock up the lid and cook for about 18 minutes under HIGH pressure
- Quick release the pressure. Open the lid and transfer the chicken to a bowl
- Shred it u using a fork
- Set your pot to sauté mode and allow the liquid to be reduced for 5 minutes
- Pour the sauce over your chicken Yum and serve with vegetables. Enjoy!

CALORIES 240; PROTEIN 24.8G; CARBOHYDRATES 17.7G; FAT 7.5G; SODIUM 134MG

CHICKEN AND POULTRY

Lime Chicken Chili

PREPARATION TIME 10 MINUTES

COOKING TIME 23 MINUTES

SERVINGS 6 PERSONS

Ingredients:

- 56.7ml cooking wine
- 100 ml organic chicken broth
- 1 onion, diced
- 6g salt
- 1.15 g paprika
- 5 garlic cloves, minced
- 15.34g lime juice
- 58 g butter
- 910g chicken thighs
- 0.54 g dried parsley
- 3 green chilies, chopped

Instructions:

- Set your Ninja-Foodi to Sauté mode and add onion and garlic
- Sauté for 3 minutes, add remaining ingredients
- Lock lid and cook on Medium-high pressure for 20 minutes
- Release pressure naturally over 10 minutes. Serve and enjoy!

CALORIES 8KCAL PROTEIN 1G CARBOHYDRATES 2G FAT 1G FIBRE 1G SODIUM 599MG SUGAR 1G

CHICKEN AND POULTRY

Chicken Piccata Pasta

PREPARATION TIME 15 MINUTES
COOKING TIME 20 MINUTES
SERVINGS 4 PERSONS

Ingredients:

- 113 g linguini, broken in half
- 473 ml chicken broth, divided
- 13.3 g olive oil
- 28 g lemon juice, plus 1 teaspoon zest, divided
- 2.29 g Sea salt, plus more for seasoning
- 4 uncooked thin-cut chicken breast fillets (110 g each)
- Ground black pepper, for seasoning
- 43 g plain flour
- 42.52 g butter, melted
- 122 g grated Parmesan cheese
- 15g capers
- 3.24 g fresh parsley, chopped

Instructions:

- Combine the pasta, 2 cups of broth, oil, 2 tablespoons of lemon juice and salt in a saucepan. Stir to combine.
- Install the pressure cap and make sure the pressure relief valve is in the seal position. select pressure and set high. set the time to 5 minutes and select start / stop to start.
- When the pressure cooker is finished, quickly release the pressure by turning the pressure relief valve to the vent position. Carefully remove the cap when the device is depressurized.
- Salt and pepper the chicken and pour in the flour, shake off the excess. Brush both sides of the chicken with melted butter.
- Add the Parmesan, capers, remaining chicken broth, remaining lemon juice and lemon zest to the cooked noodles. Place the rotating rack in the highest position in the pot over the pasta and place the chicken on the rack.
- Close the lid to grill. Select bake / roast, set the temperature to 375 ° F and the time to 15 minutes. Select start / stop to begin.

CALORIES 189 PROTEIN 6.2G CARBS 9.1G FAT 15.6G FIBRE 0.5G SODIUM 1738MG SUGAR 0.7G

BEEF, PORK AND LAMB RECIPES

BEEF, LAMB, AND PORK

Corned Beef and Cabbage

PREPARATION TIME
10 MINUTES

COOKING TIME
1 HOUR 25 MINUTES

SERVINGS
12 PERSONS

Ingredients:

- 450g salt beef brisket (with seasoning packet)
- 250 ml chicken stock
- 30 ml balsamic vinegar
- 1 onion, diced
- 7 cloves garlic, peeled
- 0.46 g dried thyme leaves
- 3 bay leaves
- 438 g gold baby potatoes, scrubbed
- 454 g carrots, peeled and cut into large pieces
- 1 head green cabbage, cored and cut in wedges

FOR GLAZE, IF DESIRED:
- 30g light brown sugar, packed
- 125ml water
- 125g Dijon mustard

Instructions:

- Place the brisket in the pan with the fat side down. Add the sachet of spices, broth, balsamic vinegar, onion, garlic, thyme and bay leaves.
- Cover the jar with a lid and close the valve.
- Set the electric pressure cooker to manual or "pressure cooker" for 1 hour 15 minutes or 75 minutes. Press Start / Stop to start the cooking cycle. Once the cycle is complete, naturally release the pressure for 10 minutes before releasing it quickly.
- Take the breast out of the pan and keep it warm. Also delete the
- Garlic and bay leaves.
- Place the potatoes, carrots and cabbage in the pot with the liquid. Cover the jar with a lid and close the valve.
- Set the electric pressure cooker to manual or "pressure cooker" for 3 minutes. Press Start / Stop to start the cooking cycle. When the cycle is complete, quickly release the pressure.
- For the frosting: In a small saucepan, heat Light brown sugar and water over medium heat until boiling. Add the mustard and continue cooking until the sauce has reduced, about 2 to 3 minutes.
- Place the salt beef brisket over the vegetables and pour the frosting over the salt beef. Put the crisp cover back on and set the Air Crisp function to 204°C. Cook for 20 minutes.

CALORIES 690 PROTEIN 58G CARBS 32G FAT 36G FIBRE 5G SODIUM 430MG SUGAR 12G

BEEF, LAMB, AND PORK

Mustard Pork Chops

PREPARATION TIME 30 MINUTES

COOKING TIME 40 MINUTES

SERVINGS 4 PERSONS

Ingredients:

- 28.35 g butter
- 30g Dijon mustard
- 4 pork chops
- Salt to taste
- black pepper as required
- 3.35 g fresh rosemary, chopped

Instructions:

- Marinate the pork chops with Dijon mustard, fresh rosemary, salt and black pepper for about 2 hours.
- Put the butter and marinated pork chops in the pot of Ninja Foodi and cover the lid.
- Press "Pressure" and cook for about 30 minutes.
- Release the pressure naturally and dish out in a platter.

CALORIES 315, PROTEIN 18.4G CARBS 1G, FAT 26.1G.

BEEF, LAMB, AND PORK

Pork Carnitas

PREPARATION TIME 10 MINUTES
COOKING TIME 25 MINUTES
SERVINGS 4 PERSONS

Ingredients:

- 910g pork butt, chopped into 50.8 mm pieces
- 6g salt
- 0.51 g oregano
- 1.02 g cumin
- 1 yellow onion, cut into half
- 6 garlic cloves, peeled and crushed
- 118 ml chicken broth

Instructions:

- Insert a pan into your Ninja Foodi and add pork. Season with salt, cumin, oregano and mix well, making sure that the pork is well seasoned
- Take the orange and squeeze the orange juice all over. Add squeezed orange to into the insert pan as well
- Add garlic cloves and onions. Pour ½ cup chicken broth into the pan
- Lock the lid of the Ninja Foodi, making sure that the valve is sealed well
- Set pressure to HIGH and let it cook for 20 minutes
- Once the timer beeps, quick release the pressure
- Open the lid and take out orange, garlic cloves, and onions. Set your Nina Foodi to Sauté mode and adjust the temperature to medium-high
- Let the liquid simmer for 10-15 minutes. After most of the liquid has been reduced, press the stop button
- Close the Ninja Foodi with "Air Crisp" lid. Pressure broil option and set timer to 8 minutes
- Take the meat and put it in wraps. Garnish with cilantro and enjoy!

BEEF, LAMB, AND PORK

Zesty Lamb Chops

PREPARATION TIME
15 MINUTES

COOKING TIME
52 MINUTES

SERVINGS
4 PERSONS

Ingredients:

- 56.7 g butter
- 43.1 lemon juice
- 4 lamb chops
- 12 g almond flour
- 236ml picante sauce

Instructions:

- Coat the chops with almond flour and keep aside.
- Press "Sauté" on Ninja Foodi and add butter and chops.
- Sauté for about 2 minutes and add picante sauce and lemon juice.
- Press "Pressure" and set the timer for 40 minutes at "Hi".
- Release the pressure naturally and dish out to serve hot.

CALORIES 284, FAT 19.5G, CARBS 1G, PROTEIN 24.8G

BEEF, LAMB, AND PORK

Beef Stroganoff

PREPARATION TIME 5 MINUTES

COOKING TIME 115 MINUTES

SERVINGS 6 PERSONS

Ingredients:

- 60 mL oil- vegetable or canola
- 1-pound beef stew meat- cut into 25.4 mm cubes
- 220 g diced white onion
- 5.69 g salt
- 110 g sour cream
- 250 g wide egg noodles
- 473 ml beef broth
- 34 ml Worcestershire sauce
- 2.33 g pepper
- 16 g flour
- 75 g sliced mushrooms
- 34 ml soy sauce
- 18 g minced garlic

Instructions:

- Turn on your Ninja Foodi and select the stir-fry function
- Add the oil and heat for 1 minute.
- Add the onion and cook until the onion is tender and translucent.
- Add the meat and season with 1 teaspoon of salt and 1 teaspoon of pepper.
- Brown the meat on all sides, stirring frequently
- Add garlic, Worcestershire sauce, mushrooms and soy sauce.
- Add the flour, making sure to coat the meat and mushrooms.
- Pour the beef broth and half a teaspoon of salt on top.
- Close the lid of the pressure cooker and put it on high pressure with the vent on the "gasket" for 10 minutes.
- When the timer beeps, turn the nozzle to "Prime" and quickly release all pressure. Open the lid and add the egg noodles.
- Close the lid and press the vent on the "gasket" at high pressure for 5 minutes When the timer rings, naturally release the pressure for 5 minutes.
- Open the lid and add ½ cup sour cream. Stir and serve!

CALORIES 499 PROTEIN 26.7G CARBS 39.5G FAT 26G FIBRE 2.6G SODIUM 1380MG SUGAR 4.2G

BEEF, LAMB, AND PORK

Crispy Pork Carnitas

PREPARATION TIME 10 MINUTES
COOKING TIME 36 MINUTES
SERVINGS 6 PERSONS

Ingredients:

- 28.35 g butter
- 2 oranges, juiced
- 907g pork shoulder
- Salt and black pepper
- 3.28 g garlic powder

Instructions:

- Apply pepper and salt to the pork for seasoning.
- Press "Sauté" on Ninja Foodi and add butter and garlic powder.
- Sauté for about 1 minute and add seasoned pork.
- Sauté for 3 minutes and pour orange juice.
- Press "Pressure" and cook for about 15 minutes on High.
- Release the pressure naturally and press "Broil".
- Broil for about 8 minutes at 375 degrees F and dish out to serve.

CALORIES 506, PROTEIN 35.9G CARBS 7.6G, FAT 36.3G

BEEF, LAMB, AND PORK

Beef Chili

PREPARATION TIME 10 MINUTES

COOKING TIME 8 MINUTES

SERVINGS 4 PERSONS

Ingredients:

- 454 g beef roast
- 473 ml beef broth
- 2 cloves of garlic, chopped
- 1 bell pepper, chopped
- 1 white onion, chopped
- 4 tomatoes, chopped
- 0.71 g dried basil
- 1.01 g dried oregano
- 3g salt
- 0.29g ground black pepper
- 58.7 g shredded cheddar cheese

Instructions:

- Place the beef roast in the Ninja Foodi pot and sprinkle with the oregano, salt, basil and ground black pepper.
- Add the broth, garlic, tomato, bell pepper and onion to the pot and close the pressure cooker lid.
- Cook on high pressure for 10 minutes. Do a quick steam release and remove the lid.
- Add the cream cheese and heavy cream and stir to blend.
- Sprinkle the cheese on top of the chili and put the air crisper top on. Use the broil function to brown the cheese for 2 minutes.

CALORIES: 282G, PROTEIN: 14G, CARBOHYDRATES: 4G, FAT: 13G, SODIUM: 1163 MG SUGAR: 2G

BEEF, LAMB, AND PORK

Beef & Broccoli

PREPARATION TIME 15 MINUTES

COOKING TIME 20 MINUTES

SERVINGS 4 PERSONS

Ingredients:

- 118 ml reduced-sodium soy sauce
- 125 ml beef broth
- 45 ml cooking sherry
- 28 g Light brown sugar
- 6 g fresh ginger, peeled, minced
- 0.45 g crushed red pepper
- 680g uncooked skirt steak
- 148g water, divided
- ½ pond broccoli florets
- 15 g corn-starch
- 4 fresh Spring onions, chopped

Instructions:

- In a medium bowl, combine soy sauce, broth, sherry, Light brown sugar, ginger and crushed red pepper. Add the steak to the mixture and marinate for 15 minutes.
- Meanwhile, add ½ cup of water and the Cook & Crisp basket to the pot. Place the broccoli in the basket.
- Install the pressure cap and make sure the pressure relief valve is in the vent position. Select STEAM and set the time to 4 minutes. Select start / stop to begin.
- When you are finished cooking, carefully remove the Snap-on cover. Remove the basket of broccoli from the pan and set aside. For the water in the pot.
- Place the steak and marinade in the pot. Install the pressure cap and make sure the pressure relief valve is in the seal position. Select pressure and set high. Set the time for 12 minutes. Select start / stop to begin.
- When you are finished quick cooking, quickly release the pressure by turning the pressure relief valve to the vent position. Carefully remove the cap when the device is depressurized.
- Combine the corn-starch and 2 tablespoons of water in a small bowl and stir until the corn-starch is dissolved. Select sear / sauté and set it to MD: HI. Select start / stop to begin. Pour the corn-starch mixture into the pot and stir until the sauce thickens.
- Add broccoli and chives to meat mixture while stirring. Once the broccoli has warmed, select start / stop for sear / sauté. switch off

CALORIES 431 PROTEIN 51.8G CARBS 19G FAT 16G FIBRE 2.3G SODIUM 1273MG SUGAR 8.2G

BEEF, LAMB, AND PORK

Rice Casserole and Minced Beef

PREPARATION TIME
5 MINUTES

COOKING TIME
25 MINUTES

SERVINGS
6 PERSONS

Ingredients:

- 454g minced Beef (96/4)
- 16.24 g Chili Powder, to spice preference
- 4.92g Garlic Powder
- 1.2g Onion Powder
- 2.30 g Smoked Paprika
- 6g Sea salt
- 1.02 g Cumin
- 0.5g Dried Oregano
- 60g Tomato Paste
- 60g Lime Juice
- 480ml Chicken Broth
- 200g bag coriander Lime Right Rice
- 112g Shredded Cheddar Cheese

Instructions:

- Cook minced beef to a high level with the Foodi stir-fry function. At the end of cooking, add the dry spices. Once the minced beef is fully cooked, add the lime juice and tomato paste and stir.
- Turn the Foodi over and add the chicken broth and the good rice. Mix well.
- Close the Foodi and cook for 5 minutes under high pressure with quick release pressure (ventilate immediately).
- Stir in the minced meat and rice before pouring the grated cheese on top. Use Food's grill function for 3 to 5 minutes until the cheese is melted and bubbly.
- Serve the minced Beef and Rice Casserole with salad

CALORIES 265 CARBS 13G PROTEIN 28G FAT 8G FIBRE 1.2G SODIUM 738MG SUGAR 0.2G

BEEF, LAMB, AND PORK

Pulled Pork

PREPARATION TIME
5 MINUTES

COOKING TIME
2 HOUR 35 MINUTES

SERVINGS
12 PERSONS

Ingredients:

- 40g pork butt
- 245 ml water
- 50 g sugar
- 14 g onion powder
- 14 g seasoned salt
- 14 g smoked paprika
- 10 g chili powder
- 6 g fine grind sea salt
- 3 g celery salt

Instructions:

- Remove the pork neck at least 30 minutes before cooking. Prepare the seasoning and rub it liberally on the pork. What is left is a dressing that can be used to season meat after cooking or stored for future use.
- Add 1 cup of water to the inner pot and place the pork fat side up on the wire rack or in a loop and place it in the pot. You want the pork to rise above the liquid. Replace the pressure cap and turn the valve to seal. Cook on high pressure for 90 minutes to make a 450g pork butt. See the tips for cooking tips for small pieces of pork.
- When the time is up, naturally releasing the pressure until the pen drops. Open the lid and take out the grill with the pork. Remove the liquid from the pan. I lift it up and store it in the fridge for other uses or to add fat and juice to the meat after pulling it.
- Return pork to inner pot. I put it straight into the inner pot so that there was enough space between the crispy lid and the top of the pork. Close lid to broil and aerate at 150 ° C for 1 hour. Check it after 30 minutes to make sure the top isn't getting too dark.
- Remove the pork with meat forks or grating forks and place it on a cutting board to cool. When it is cold enough to handle, remove the meat and cut it into pieces of the desired size. The meat should come off very easily. Otherwise, remove the crispy top and pc for an additional 20-30 minutes. If you are using a bone-in stump of pork, remove the bone and discard it.
- Season the pulled pork with an extra touch or add your favourite barbecue sauce.
- Serve and enjoy!

CALORIES 327 PROTEIN 48G CARBS 6G FAT 16G FIBRE 1G SODIUM 2201MG SUGAR 4G

BEEF, LAMB, AND PORK

Beefy Stew

PREPARATION TIME 10 MINUTES

COOKING TIME 20 MINUTES

SERVINGS 2 PERSONS

Ingredients:

- 14.79 ml vegetable oil
- 1 onion, chopped
- 2 cloves of garlic, minced
- 340g beef stew meat, cut into chunks
- 3.05g ground cumin
- 0.18 g saffron threads
- 1.59 g turmeric
- 0.66 g ground cinnamon
- 0.51 g ground allspice
- Salt to taste
- Pepper as required
- 28.1 g tomato paste
- 1/2 can split peas, rinsed and drained
- 475 ml bone broth
- 1 can crushed tomatoes
- 28.7 g lemon juice, freshly squeezed

Instructions:

- Press the sauté button on the Ninja Foodi. Heat the oil and sauté the onion and garlic until fragrant. Add cumin, saffron, turmeric, cinnamon, and allspice. Stir in the beef and sear button for 3 minutes. Season with salt and pepper to taste.
- Pour in the rest of the ingredients.
- Install pressure lid. Close Ninja Foodi, press the pressure button, choose high settings, and set time to 20 minutes.
- Once done cooking, do a quick release.
- Serve and enjoy.

CALORIES: 466; CARBOHYDRATES: 36G; PROTEIN: 49G; FAT: 14G

BEEF, LAMB, AND PORK

Lamb with Mint

PREPARATION TIME 55 MINUTES
COOKING TIME 60 MINUTES
SERVINGS 6 PERSONS

Ingredients:

- 1.2kg half leg of lamb (raw)
- 3 cloves of garlic (optional - peeled and thinly sliced)
- 25g small bunch fresh mint (finely sliced)
- 20ml rapeseed or vegetable oil
- To taste salt and freshly ground black pepper
- 25g thickening gravy granules

Instructions:

- Place the lamb on a suitable board (for the meat). If using garlic, prick the meat (about 30 times) with the tip of a sharp knife to make small incisions in the meat
- Place a slice of garlic in each slit and season the lamb with salt and freshly ground black pepper.
- Pour 200 ml of cold water into the pan of your Ninja Foodi.
- Place the lamb in the Cook & Crisp basket and place the basket in the pan (you may need to cut the bone if it is too long for the basket)
- Install the pressure cap and make sure the relief valve is in the seal position. Select pressure and set high. Set the time to 32 minutes. Select start / stop to begin
- When pressure cooking is complete, naturally release the pressure for 2 minutes. After 2 minutes, quickly release any remaining pressure by gently moving the pressure release to the wind position. Remove the cap when the device is depressurized.
- Brush the lamb with rapeseed / vegetable oil.
- Close the lid to grill. Select air crisp, set the temperature to 200 ° C and the time to 8 minutes. Select start / stop to begin. When the cooking process is complete, take the basket out of the pot and cover it loosely with foil on a plate.
- To make a sauce, add the sauce granules to the pot with the cooking liquid and stir them with a whisk (or a spoon). At this point you can add a little more water, broth, or even a drop of wine if you want. Install the pressure cap and make sure the pressure relief valve is in the seal position
- Select pressure and set it to low. Set the time to 3 minutes. Select start / stop to begin
- When pressure cooking is complete, quickly release the pressure by setting the pressure release to the vent position. Carefully remove the cap when the pressure is released.
- Stir the sauce and adjust the consistency with a little more liquid (water, broth or wine) if it is too thick. Pour the sauce through a sieve into a saucepan or saucepan and add the finely chopped fresh mint.
- To serve, cut the resting lamb into slices and place it on a warm serving platter. Top with salsa and serve with

CALORIES 395 PROTEIN 60G CARBS 3.5G FAT 13.6G FIBRE 1.2G SODIUM 0MG SUGAR 0.2G

BEEF, LAMB, AND PORK

Sweet and Savoury Pork fillet steak

PREPARATION TIME
5 MINUTES

COOKING TIME
5 MINUTES

SERVINGS
4 PERSONS

Ingredients:

- 122.6 kg pork fillet steak
- 621 ml pork gravy
- 125 ml water
- 6 carrots (cut into 2-3 pieces each)
- 5 red potatoes (large and cut into 5 or 6 pieces each)
- 100 g Light brown sugar
- 56 g butter (salted and cut into 8 pieces)
- 3 sprigs thyme (fresh)
- 1.5 g salt
- 0.60 g pepper

Instructions:

- Take the pork fillet steak from the package and season lightly with S&P. Make 1-inch cuts on the pork tenderloin; anything between 6 and 8 will work.
- Spread out the grooves a little, then put a piece of butter in each groove.
- Place the pork tenderloin on the Ninja Foodi. Add the potatoes and carrots around the pork tenderloin.
- Add the Light brown sugar and try to place it in the center of the pork tenderloin.
- In a separate bowl, add 118ml of water to 2 cans of pork sauce and mix well. Pour the pork sauce mixture over the pork tenderloin.
- Cover with sprigs of fresh thyme. Add the pressure cooker lid.
- Close and set to high manual power for 5 minutes.
- When the timer expires, release natural pressure for 10 minutes, then quickly release remaining pressure.
- Take the net from the Ninja Foodi and save. Open, place on a plate and pour the sauce over the pork tenderloin and vegetables.

CALORIES 695 PROTEIN 41G CARBS 88G FAT 20G FIBRE 7G SODIUM 1238MG SUGAR 40G

BEEF, LAMB, AND PORK

Roasted Lamb Cutlet

PREPARATION TIME 5 MINUTES

COOKING TIME 5 MINUTES

SERVINGS 6 PERSONS

Ingredients:

- 16 lamb cutlet rib cutlet/loin cutlet
- 9.17 g Sea salt
- 1.17 g black pepper
- 0.90 g cayenne pepper or to taste
- 3.28 g granulated garlic
- 1.2g onion powder
- 56 g Whole Greek yogurt/honey

Instructions:

- Season the lamb with salt, black pepper, cayenne pepper, granulated garlic and onion powder.
- Brush the lamb with 56 g honey/plain Greek yogurt
- Grill or roast the lamb for 4 to 7 minutes of Ninja Foodi you have. Turn if needed

CALORIES 1265 PROTEIN 118G CARBS 3G FAT 66G FIBRE 1.2G SODIUM 738MG SUGAR 0.2G

BEEF, LAMB, AND PORK

Pepper Garlic Pork Fillet Steak

PREPARATION TIME
5 MINUTES

COOKING TIME
10 MINUTES

SERVINGS
6 PERSONS

Ingredients:

- 1 pork fillet steak
- 25.8g minced garlic
- 250 ml of beef broth
- 128 g honey
- 15 ml balsamic glaze
- 7 g ground pepper
- 12g Light brown sugar
- 24 g corn starch
- 60 ml Worcestershire sauce

Instructions:

- Combine pepper, garlic and Light brown sugar in a small bowl.
- Rub this mixture on the net and keep it.
- In your Ninja Foodi casserole, combine 1 cup of beef broth, honey, balsamic glaze and Worcestershire sauce.
- Whip the contents of Ninja Foodi: use a silicone whisk to avoid scratching the pot Give the net to the Ninja Foodi
- Cover, close and put in high pressure cooking for 5 minutes, put the valve on "seal"
- When the timer expires, release natural pressure for 10 minutes, then quickly release remaining pressure. Then remove the net from Ninja Foodi and save
- Combine the cornflour and the rest of the broth in a glass, shake until completely dissolved.
- Turn the Ninja Foodi stir-fry for 5 minutes and add the cornflour mixture, beating until thickened
- Cut the fillet into slices, serve and pour the sauce over it.

CALORIES 265 PROTEIN 7.8G CARBS 53G FAT 1.6G FIBRE 0.2G SODIUM 338MG SUGAR 43.2G

BEEF, LAMB, AND PORK

Simple Pressure-Cooked Lamb Meat

PREPARATION TIME 5 MINUTES
COOKING TIME 55 MINUTES
SERVINGS 4 PERSONS

Ingredients:

- 28.35g butter
- 1.59g turmeric powder
- 450g ground lamb meat
- 52g onions, chopped
- 6g salt
- 8.62g garlic, minced
- 1.69g ground coriander
- 3.58g cayenne pepper
- 5.27g ginger, minced
- 2.03g cumin powder

Instructions:

- Set your Ninja Foodi to sauté mode and add garlic, ginger, and onions
- sauté for 3 minutes and add ground meat, spices
- Lock lid and cook on high pressure for 20 minutes
- Release pressure naturally over 10 minutes. Serve and enjoy!

CALORIES 276 PROTEIN 10G CARB 16G FAT 19G FIBRE 3G SODIUM 728MG

BEEF, LAMB, AND PORK

Rosemary Anchovy Lamb

PREPARATION TIME
5-10 MINUTES

COOKING TIME
95 MINUTES

SERVINGS
8 PERSONS

Ingredients:

- 473ml chicken broth
- 6 anchovies' fillets, chopped
- 8.87g olive oil
- 4 pounds bone-in lamb shoulder
- 1 rosemary sprig
- 1.01g dried oregano
- 2.8 g garlic, minced
- Salt, to taste preference

Instructions:

- Take Ninja Foodi multi-cooker, arrange it over a cooking platform, and open the top lid.
- In the pot, add the oil; Select "Sear/Sauté" mode and select "Md: Hi" pressure level. Press "Stop/Start." After about 4-5 minutes, the oil will start simmering.
- Add the lamb shoulder and stir-cook for about 2-3 minutes to brown evenly. Set aside.
- In the pot, add the broth, anchovies, and garlic puree. Add the lamb shoulder on top and sprinkle with oregano, rosemary, and salt. Stir the mixture.
- Secure the multi-cooker by locking it with the pressure lid; ensure to keep the pressure release valve locked/sealed.
- Select "Pressure" mode and select the "Hi" pressure level. Then, set timer to 90 minutes and press "Stop/Start"; it will start the cooking process by building up inside pressure.
- When the timer goes off, naturally release inside pressure for about 8-10 minutes. Then, quick-release pressure by adjusting the pressure valve to the Vent.
- Open the lid, slice the lamb into small pieces, and serve warm.

CALORIES: 456 PROTEIN: 48G CARBOHYDRATES: 3G FAT: 19.5G FIBRE: 0G SODIUM: 958MG

FISH AND SEA FOOD RECIPES

SEAFOOD AND FISH

Fish and Grits

PREPARATION TIME 10 MINUTES

COOKING TIME 30 MINUTES

SERVINGS 2 PERSONS

Ingredients:

- 700 ml chicken broth
- 240 ml Double cream
- 172g stone ground grits
- 28.35 g butter
- 6g salt
- 2 pieces tilapia fish
- 8g blackened or Cajun seasoning
- vegetable oil in a spray bottle

Instructions:

- Pour the chicken broth, Double cream, groats, salt and butter into the Ninja Foodi pressure cooker. Stir. Cover with the pressure cooker lid. Make sure the valve is set to "Seal".
- Cook on high pressure for 8 minutes. After 8 minutes, let Ninja Foodi release naturally for 10 minutes. Press Cancel and release the remaining pressure by turning the valve to "Vent".
- Meanwhile, season the fish with charred or Cajun seasoning by basting the fish first, then rubbing the seasonings on both sides of the fish.
- Once all the pressure is released, open the food and stir in the grains. Place a piece of sturdy foil over the grains to cover them. Place the seasoned fish on the foil. Spray again with oil.
- Close the Air Crisp lid of the Ninja Foodi. Bake at 400 degrees Fahrenheit for 10 minutes or until the fish can easily peel off with a fork.
- Serve the fish on semolina and enjoy

CALORIES 787 PROTEIN 32G CARBS 72G FAT 47.5G FIBRE 7G SODIUM 2510MG SUGAR 1.1G

SEAFOOD AND FISH

Sweet 'n Spicy Mahi-mahi

PREPARATION TIME 10 MINUTES

COOKING TIME 10 MINUTES

SERVINGS 2 PERSONS

Ingredients:

- 2 6-oz mahi-mahi fillets
- Salt, to taste
- Black pepper, to taste
- 1-2 cloves garlic, minced or crushed
- 1" piece ginger, finely grated
- ½ lime, juiced
- 40ml honey
- 6g Nanami togarashi
- 30g sriracha
- 16 ml orange juice

Instructions:

- In a heatproof dish that fits inside the Ninja Foodi, mix well orange juice, sriracha, nanami togarashi, honey lime juice, ginger, and garlic.
- Season mahi-mahi with pepper and salt. Place in bowl of sauce and cover well in sauce. Seal dish securely with foil.
- Install pressure lid and place valve to vent position.
- Add a cup of water in Ninja Foodi, place trivet, and add dish of mahi-mahi on trivet.
- Close Ninja Foodi, press steam button and set time to 10 minutes.
- Once done cooking, do a quick release. Serve and enjoy.

CALORIES: 200; CARBOHYDRATES: 20.1G; PROTEIN: 28.1G; FAT: 0.8G

SEAFOOD AND FISH

Creamy Herb 'n Parm Salmon

PREPARATION TIME
5 MINUTES

COOKING TIME
10 MINUTES

SERVINGS
2 PERSONS

Ingredients:

- 2 frozen salmon filets
- 118 ml water
- 7.5g minced garlic
- 60g double cream
- 89.9g cheese grated
- 3.04g chopped fresh chives
- 3.80g chopped fresh parsley
- 3.14g fresh dill
- 40.87ml fresh lemon juice
- Salt and pepper to taste

Instructions:

- Add water and trivet in pot. Place fillets on top of trivet.
- Install pressure lid. Close Ninja Foodi, press pressure button, choose high settings, and set time to 4 minutes.
- Once done cooking, do a quick release.
- Transfer salmon to a serving plate. And remove trivet.
- Press stop and then press sauté button on Ninja Foodi. Stir in double cream once water begins to boil. Boil for 3 minutes. Press stop and then stir in lemon juice, parmesan cheese, dill, parsley, and chives. Season with pepper and salt to taste. Pour over salmon.
- Serve and enjoy.

CALORIES: 423; CARBOHYDRATES: 6.4G; PROTEIN: 43.1G; FAT: 25.0G

SEAFOOD AND FISH

Pasta 'n Tuna Bake

PREPARATION TIME
5 MINUTES

COOKING TIME
10 MINUTES

SERVINGS
2 PERSONS

Ingredients:

- 1 can cream-of-mushroom soup
- 375 ml water
- 150g macaroni pasta
- 1 can tuna
- 72.5 g frozen peas
- 3g salt
- 2.30 g pepper
- 117 g shredded cheddar cheese

Instructions:

- Mix soup and water in Ninja Foodi.
- Add remaining ingredients except for cheese. Stir.
- Install pressure lid.
- Close Ninja Foodi, press pressure button, choose high settings, and set time to 4 minutes.
- Once done cooking, do a quick release.
- Remove pressure lid.
- Stir in cheese and roast for 5 minutes.
- Serve and enjoy.

CALORIES: 378; CARBOHYDRATES: 34.0G; PROTEIN: 28.0G; FAT: 14.1G

SEAFOOD AND FISH

Shrimp Risotto

PREPARATION TIME
20 MINUTES

COOKING TIME
10 MINUTES

SERVINGS
8 PERSONS

Ingredients:

- 26.6 g olive oil
- 26 g diced onions
- 6.56g minced garlic
- 65 ml white wine
- 225g arborio rice
- 700ml chicken broth or chicken stock
- 6g salt
- 1.17g black pepper
- 67 g shredded Parmesan cheese
- 454 g shrimp

Instructions:

- Start by sautéing the onions in olive oil for a few minutes until they are translucent and tender.
- Then add the rice and chopped garlic and sauté for a few minutes until the rice is toasted.
- Add the wine and mix well. You really want to get all those little bits of rice, onion, and garlic sticking to the bottom of the pot. Then add your chicken broth, cheese, salt and black pepper. Mix well. Put the lid in the pressure cooker and set the time to 8 minutes. (High) When the time is up, release the fan by opening the air vent.
- Mix well after opening the lid.
- Add the shrimp and press the sear function to sear the Ninja Foodi. Sauté for a few minutes until the shrimp are opaque.
- Serve, serve and enjoy!

CALORIES 265 PROTEIN 18.2G CARBS 31G FIBRE 1.2G FAT 5.6G SODIUM 738MG SUGAR 0.2G

SEAFOOD AND FISH

Hearty Swordfish Meal

PREPARATION TIME
20 MINUTES

COOKING TIME
10 MINUTES

SERVINGS
4 PERSONS

Ingredients:

- 5 swordfish fillets
- 125 ml of melted clarified butter
- 6 garlic cloves, chopped
- 15 ml black pepper

Instructions:

- Take a mixing bowl and add garlic, clarified butter, black pepper
- Take a parchment paper and add the fillet
- Cover and wrap the fish
- Keep repeating until the fillets are wrapped up
- Transfer wrapped fish to Ninja Foodi pot and lock lid
- Allow them to cook for 2 and a ½ hour at high pressure
- Release the pressure naturally. Serve and enjoy!

CALORIES: 379 FAT: 26G CARBOHYDRATES: 1G PROTEIN: 34G

SEAFOOD AND FISH

Salmon Stew

PREPARATION TIME
8 MINUTES

COOKING TIME
16 MINUTES

SERVINGS
3 PERSONS

Ingredients:

- 237 ml homemade fish broth
- Salt to taste
- black pepper as required
- 1 chopped onion
- 4.54g salmon fillet, cubed
- 14.17 g butter

Instructions:

- Season the salmon fillets with salt and black pepper.
- Press "Sauté" on Ninja Foodi and add butter and onions.
- Sauté for about 3 minutes and add salmon and fish broth.
- Lock the lid and set the Ninja Foodi to "Pressure" for about 8 minutes.
- Release the pressure naturally and dish out to serve hot.

CALORIES 272, PROTEIN 32.1G CARBS 4.4G, FAT 14.2G,

SEAFOOD AND FISH

Chili Lime Salmon

PREPARATION TIME
5 MINUTES

COOKING TIME
5 MINUTES

SERVINGS
2 PERSONS

Ingredients:

- 118 ml water
- 24g butter
- 76.6 g lime juice
- 450g Salmon, de boned
- 1.36 g ground chili powder

Instructions:

- Add the salmon into the cook and crisp basket and place the basket inside the Ninja Foodi.
- Sprinkle the chili powder over the top of the salmon and then add the water, butter and lime juice around the filets.
- Place the pressure cooker lid on top of the pot and close the pressure valve to the seal position. Set the pressure cooker function to high heat and set the timer for 3 minutes.
- Once the cooking cycle is complete, release the pressure quickly by carefully opening the steamer valve. Enjoy while hot

CALORIES: 349G, PROTEIN: 44G, CARBOHYDRATES: 8G, FAT: 17G, SODIUM: 566G SUGAR: 1G

SEAFOOD AND FISH

Salmon With Orange-ginger Sauce

PREPARATION TIME
5 MINUTES

COOKING TIME
15 MINUTES

SERVINGS
2 PERSONS

Ingredients:

- 454g salmon
- 16.00g dark soy sauce
- 3.52 g minced ginger
- 2.8 g minced garlic
- 6g salt
- 3.5g ground pepper
- 20g low sugar marmalade

Instructions:

- In a heatproof pan that fits inside your Ninja Foodi, add salmon.
- Mix all the sauce ingredients and pour over the salmon. Allow to marinate for 15-30 minutes. Cover pan with foil securely.
- Put 2 cups of water in Ninja Foodi and add trivet.
- Place the pan of salmon on trivet.
- Install pressure lid. Close Ninja Foodi, press pressure button, choose low settings, and set time to 5 minutes.
- Once done cooking, do a quick release. Serve and enjoy.

CALORIES: 177; PROTEIN: 24.0G; CARBOHYDRATES: 8.8G; FAT: 5.0G

SEAFOOD AND FISH

Simple Fish Stew

PREPARATION TIME
10 MINUTES

COOKING TIME
20 MINUTES

SERVINGS
2 PERSONS

Ingredients:

- 750 ml fish stock
- 1 onion, diced
- 250 ml broccoli, chopped
- 450 ml celery stalks, chopped
- 1 carrot, sliced
- 450g white fish fillets, chopped
- 1.25 ml pepper
- 375 ml cauliflower, diced
- 2.5 ml salt
- 1.25 ml garlic powder
- 250 ml heavy cream
- 1 bay leaf
- 30 ml butter

Instructions:

- Set your Ninja Foodi to Saute mode and add butter, let it melt
- Add onion and carrots, cook for 3 minutes
- Stir in remaining ingredients
- Lock lid and cook on HIGH pressure for 4 minutes
- Naturally, release pressure over 10 minutes. Discard bay leaf
- Serve and enjoy!

CALORIES 346 PROTEIN 42G CARBS 20G FAT 8G FIBRE 11G SUGARS 17G

SEAFOOD AND FISH

Veggie Fish Soup

PREPARATION TIME: 10 MINUTES
COOKING TIME: 10 MINUTES
SERVINGS: 4 PERSONS

Ingredients:

- 450g cod
- 1,419ml chicken broth
- 2 cloves of garlic, chopped
- 1 carrot, chopped
- 1 Bell pepper, chopped
- 1 sweet potato, peeled, diced
- 2 celery stalks, chopped
- ½ white onion, chopped
- 1.5g salt
- 0.36g ground black pepper
- 58.7 g shredded cheddar cheese

Instructions:

- Add all the ingredients to the pot and place the pressure cooker lid on the Ninja Foodi.
- Cook on high pressure for 10 minutes. Do a quick steam release and remove the lid.
- Remove the chicken from the pot and shred the chicken using two forks.
- Serve while hot or freeze to use at a later date.

CALORIES: 250G, PROTEIN: 36G, CARBOHYDRATES: 4G, FAT: 0G, SODIUM: 438MG, SUGAR: 2G

SEAFOOD AND FISH

Garlic Sock-Eye Salmon

PREPARATION TIME
5 MINUTES

COOKING TIME
15 MINUTES

SERVINGS
4 PERSONS

Ingredients:

- 4 sockeye salmon fillets
- 5 ml Dijon mustard
- 1.25 ml garlic, minced
- 1.25 ml onion powder
- 1.25 ml lemon pepper
- 2.5 ml garlic powder
- 1.25 ml salt
- 30 ml olive oil
- 375 ml of water

Instructions:

- Take a bowl and add mustard, lemon juice, onion powder, lemon pepper, garlic powder, salt, olive oil
- Brush spice mix over salmon
- Add water to ninja Foodi cooker
- Place rack and place salmon fillets on rack
- Lock lid and cook on LOW pressure for 7 minutes
- Quick release pressure. Serve and enjoy!

CALORIES: 353 PROTEIN: 40G CARBOHYDRATES: 0.6G FAT: 25G

SEAFOOD AND FISH

Cherry Tomato Mackerel

PREPARATION TIME
10 MINUTES

COOKING TIME
20 MINUTES

SERVINGS
4 PERSONS

Ingredients:

- 4 Mackerel fillets
- 1.25 ml onion powder
- 1.25 ml lemon powder
- 1.25 ml garlic powder
- 2.5 ml salt
- 450 ml cherry tomatoes
- 45 ml melted butter
- 375 ml of water
- 15 ml black olives

Instructions:

- Grease baking dish and arrange cherry tomatoes at the bottom of the dish
- Top with fillets sprinkle all spices
- Drizzle melted butter over and add water to your Ninja Foodi
- Lower rack in Ninja Foodi and place baking dish on top of the rack
- Lock lid and cook on LOW pressure for 7 minutes
- Quick release pressure, serve and enjoy!

CALORIES: 325 PROTEIN: 21G CARBOHYDRATES: 2G FAT: 24G

SEAFOOD AND FISH

Shrimp Zoodles

PREPARATION TIME
15 MINUTES

COOKING TIME
10 MINUTES

SERVINGS
2 PERSONS

Ingredients:

- 1 litre zoodles
- 2.5 ml paprika
- 30 ml Ghee
- 250 ml vegetable stock
- 15 ml basil, chopped
- 2 garlic cloves, minced
- 30 ml olive oil
- ½ lemon

Instructions:

- Set your Ninja Foodi to sauté mode and add ghee, let it heat up
- Add olive oil as well
- Add garlic and cook for 1 minute
- Add lemon juice, shrimp and cook for 1 minute
- Stir in rest of the ingredients and lock lid, cook on LOW pressure for 5 minutes
- Quick release pressure and serve Enjoy!

CALORIES: 277 PROTEIN: 27G CARBOHYDRATES: 5G FAT: 6G.

SEAFOOD AND FISH

Garlic And Lemon Prawn Delight

PREPARATION TIME
5 MINUTES

COOKING TIME
5 MINUTES

SERVINGS
4 PERSONS

Ingredients:

- 27g olive oil
- 458g prawns
- 17.24g garlic, minced
- 158 ml fish stock
- 14.17g butter
- 28.7 g lemon juice
- 6fg lemon zest
- Salt to taste
- Pepper as required

Instructions:

- Set your Ninja Foodi to sauté mode and add butter and oil, let it heat up
- Stir in remaining ingredients. Lock lid and cook on LOW pressure for 5 minutes
- Quick release pressure. Serve and enjoy!

CALORIES: 338KCAL PROTEIN: 40G CARBOHYDRATES: 1G FAT: 18G SODIUM: 1544MG

SEAFOOD AND FISH

Breath-taking Cod Fillets

PREPARATION TIME
10 MINUTES

COOKING TIME
5-10 MINUTES

SERVINGS
4 PERSONS

Ingredients:

- 454g frozen cod fish fillets
- 2 garlic cloves, halved
- 200 ml chicken broth
- 100.5 g packed parsley
- 6.08g oregano
- 8.75g almonds, sliced
- 58 g paprika

Instructions:

- Take the fish out of the freezer and let it defrost
- Take a food processor and stir in garlic, oregano, parsley, paprika, 1 tablespoon almond and process. Set your Ninja Foodi to "sauté" mode and add olive oil, let it heat up
- Add remaining almonds and toast, transfer to a towel. Pour broth in a pot and add herb mixture
- Cut fish into 4 pieces and place in a steamer basket, transfer steamer basket to the pot
- Lock lid and cook on high pressure for 3 minutes. Quick release pressure once has done
- Serve steamed fish by pouring over the sauce. Enjoy!

CALORIES: 294KCAL PROTEIN: 30G FAT: 18G SODIUM: 385MG

SEAFOOD AND FISH

Flaky Fish with Ginger

PREPARATION TIME
10 MINUTES

COOKING TIME
15 MINUTES

SERVINGS
2 PERSONS

Ingredients:

- 453.59 of g halibut fillet, skin removed
- 5.9g salt
- 2.00g fresh ginger, sliced thinly
- 3.25g green onion
- 15ml dark soy sauce
- 15.77ml peanut oil
- 4.5g sesame oil

Instructions:

- Place the Foodi Cook &Crisp reversible rack inside the ceramic pot.
- Pour a cup of water in the pot.
- Season the halibut fillets with salt to taste.
- Place in a heat-proof ceramic dish. Drizzle with the rest of the ingredients.
- Place the ceramic dish with the fish inside on the reversible rack.
- Close the pressure lid and set the vent to SEAL.
- Press the Steam button and adjust the cooking time to 15 minutes.
- Do quick pressure release.

CALORIES: 352; PROTEIN: 48.1G; CARBOHYDRATES: 2G; FAT: 16.8G; SODIUM: 1908MG SUGAR: 0.2G;

DESSERT RECIPES

DESSERT RECIPES

Meatloaf

PREPARATION TIME 10 MINUTES
COOKING TIME 35 MINUTES
SERVINGS 6 PERSONS

Ingredients:

- 450 ml, ground beef
- 250 ml, ground chicken
- 2 eggs
- 60 ml, fresh dill
- 5 ml ground black pepper
- 15 ml, salt
- 5 ml, cilantro
- 15 ml, basil
- 2.5 ml, paprika
- 15 ml, butter
- Breadcrumbs

Instructions:

- Combine chicken with ground beef in a mixing bowl.
- Add egg, salt, ground black pepper, paprika, butter, cilantro, and basil.
- Chop the dill and add it to the ground meat mixture and stir using your hand.
- Place the meat mixture on an aluminium foil and add breadcrumbs before wrapping it.
- Place it in a pressure cooker and close its lid. Cook the dish on sauté mode and cook for 40 minutes.
- When the cooking time ends, remove your meatloaf from the cooker and allow it to cool.
- Unwrap the foil, slice it, and serve.

CALORIES 173, PROTEIN 16 G, CARBOHYDRATES 0.81 G, FATS 11.5 G

DESSERT RECIPES

Kale And Almonds Mix

PREPARATION TIME MINUTES

COOKING TIME MINUTES

SERVINGS PERSONS

Ingredients:

- 250 ml of water
- 1 big kale bunch, chopped
- 15 ml balsamic vinegar
- 30 ml olive oil
- 3 garlic cloves, minced
- 1 small yellow onion, chopped
- 75 ml toasted almonds

Instructions:

- Set your Ninja Foodi on sauté mode and add oil, let it heat up
- Stir in onion and cook for 3 minutes. Add garlic, water, kale, and stir
- Lock lid and cook on High pressure for 4 minutes. Quick release pressure
- Add salt, pepper, vinegar, almonds and toss well. Serve and enjoy!

CALORIES: 140 PROTEIN: 3G CARBOHYDRATES: 5G FAT: 6G

DESSERT RECIPES

Apple Pie Filling

PREPARATION TIME 10 MINUTES

COOKING TIME 10 MINUTES

SERVINGS 8 PERSONS

Ingredients:

- 8 medium-sized apples
- 1 orange zest & juice
- 100 g sugar
- 1 tsp vanilla extract
- Spice Blend
- 4.20g cinnamon
- 2.29 g fine grind sea salt
- 0.59 g nutmeg
- 0.51 g allspice

Instructions:

- Grate and squeeze the orange into the inner pot of the Ninja Foodi. Put the sugar in the inner pot.
- Core, peel and cut the apples into quarters. Put them in the inner pot. Stir several times as you add the apples to prevent them from turning brown.
- Replace the pressure cap and turn the valve to seal. Set the pressure to high and the time to zero minutes. Once the stove has increased its pressure, it will beep to indicate that it is ready. Get instant approval.
- Stir the apples and cut them into small pieces if necessary. I use my Mix 'N Chop and it works great.
- Add the vanilla extract. Mix the spices and season to taste. Add more spices and / or sugar as you wish. Let it cool until you are ready to use your cake filling.

CALORIES 175 PROTEIN 1G CARBS 46G FAT 1G FIBRE 1.2G SODIUM 138MG SUGAR 28G

DESSERT RECIPES

Cheese Dredged Cauliflower Snack

PREPARATION TIME
10 MINUTES

COOKING TIME
30 MINUTES

SERVINGS
4 PERSONS

Ingredients:

- 15.79 g mustard
- 1 head cauliflower
- 14.79ml avocado mayonnaise
- 45 g parmesan cheese, grated
- 59.91 g butter, cut into small pieces

Instructions:

- Set your Ninja Foodi to Sauté mode and add butter and cauliflower
- Sauté for 3 minutes. Add remaining ingredients and stir
- Lock lid and cook on high pressure for 30 minutes. Release pressure naturally over 10 minutes
- Serve and enjoy!

CALORIES: 155 PROTEIN: 6G CARBOHYDRATES: 4G FAT: 13G

DESSERT RECIPES

Coconutty-blueberry Cake

PREPARATION TIME
15 MINUTES

COOKING TIME
10 MINUTES

SERVINGS
2 PERSONS

Ingredients:

- 30.8 g coconut flour
- 2 large eggs
- 2 g baking soda
- 59 ml coconut milk
- 0.5g lemon zest

Instructions:

- Combine all ingredients in a mixing bowl.
- Pour into two mugs. Cover top of mugs securely with foil.
- 3Place a steam rack in the Ninja Foodi and pour a cup of water.
- Place the mug on the steam rack.
- Install pressure lid. Close the lid, press the steam button, and adjust the time to 10 minutes.
- Do a natural pressure release.

CALORIES: 259; PROTEIN: 7.2G; CARBOHYDRATES: 10.3G; FAT: 20.9G

DESSERT RECIPES

Cauliflower Patties

PREPARATION TIME 10 MINUTES
COOKING TIME 25 MINUTES
SERVINGS 8 PERSONS

Ingredients:

- 1 chili pepper, chopped
- 2.5 ml garlic powder
- 3 whole eggs
- 60 ml cheddar cheese
- 450 ml cauliflower, chopped
- 60 ml whole mozzarella cheese
- Salt and pepper to taste
- 175 ml olive oil

Instructions:

- Cut cauliflower into small florets, remove leaves and cut out a core
- Add 250 ml water to Ninja Food, transfer florets to steamer basket and place it on a trivet in your Ninja Foodi. Lock lid and cook on high pressure for 5 minutes
- Mash steamed cauliflower and dry them, add shredded cheese, eggs, chili, salt and pepper
- Mix well and shape into flat patties
- Heat up oil in your Ninja Foodi and set to Sauté mode, shallow fry patties until crisp on both sides. Serve and enjoy!

CALORIES: 550 PROTEIN: 13G CARBOHYDRATES: 5G FAT: 54G

DESSERT RECIPES

Grape Jelly

PREPARATION TIME
10 MINUTES

COOKING TIME
20 MINUTES

SERVINGS
5 PERSONS

Ingredients:

- 1800 g Concord grapes
- 1350 g seedless grapes
- 118 ml water
- 340 grams liquid pectin
- 50 g sugar

Instructions:

- Wash and sort the grapes thoroughly. Discard the stems. Add grapes in the pot and use the immersion blender to crush them. Add the water.
- Press "Function" and turn the dial to the "pressure cook" function. Press "Temp" and use the dial to adjust the temperature to High.
- Press "Time" and use the dial to adjust the temperature to 3 minutes. Press "Start/Stop" to start cooking.
- When done, perform a natural release of 15 minutes. When the pressure releases open the lid and use a fine mesh sieve lined with a damp cheesecloth to strain the juice.
- Return juice to the pot and add the sugar.
- Press "Function" and turn the dial to the "Sear/Sauté" function. Press "Temp" and use the dial to adjust the temperature to High.
- Press the "start/stop" button to start cooking. Bring to a boil then add in the pectin. Boil for 1 minute.
- Turn off the heat and skim off the foam. Empty into hot, sterilized air-tight glass jars.
- Fill about to 1" lower than the lid. Seal and allow to cool for 24 hours.

CALORIES: 23 PROTEIN: 0G CARBOHYDRATES: 6G   FAT: 0 FIBRE: 0G

DESSERT RECIPES

Rice Pudding

PREPARATION TIME: 5 MINUTES
COOKING TIME: 15 MINUTES
SERVINGS: 10 PERSONS

Ingredients:

- 185 g White Rice
- 354 g Jasmine Tea brewed
- 1.32 g Cinnamon
- 0.59 g Nutmeg
- 0.75 g sea salt
- 3.92g Cardamom
- 396.89 g Sweetened Condensed Milk
- 72.5 g' raisins I used golden
- 1 egg lightly beaten
- 121 g Single cream or heavy whipping cream
- 4.93ml vanilla extract

Instructions:

- Prepare jasmine tea. Please see the post for different ways of brewing tea. Pour 1½ cups of jasmine tea into the Ninja Foodi's inner pot.
- Add rinsed jasmine or white rice to the inner pot.
- Add the spices; cinnamon, nutmeg, sea salt and cardamom.
- Stir and close the lid. Make sure the valve is tight. Put at high pressure for 5 minutes. Let Ninja Foodi naturally deflate for 5 minutes, then manually release the remaining pressure. Remove the cap.
- Turn the sauce over high heat and add the sweetened condensed milk, 1 lightly beaten egg and ½ cup of golden raisins. Stir frequently for about 5 minutes.
- Add heavy, Single cream or Double cream until the jasmine pudding is the desired consistency. Turn off the Ninja Foodi.
- Add the vanilla extract, mix. Serve and enjoy!
- Serve the Rice Pudding with some snacks

CALORIES 241 PROTEIN 8G CARBS 43G FAT 6G FIBRE 1G SODIUM 98MG SUGAR 22G

DESSERT RECIPES

Strawberry Chocolate Chip Mug Cake

PREPARATION TIME
10 MINUTES

COOKING TIME
10 MINUTES

SERVINGS
2 PERSONS

Ingredients:

- 64 g almond flour
- 2 eggs
- 236.59ml maple syrup
- 4.9ml vanilla
- 0.75 g salt
- 8 large strawberries, chopped
- 39.98g dark chocolate chips

Instructions:

- Mix all the ingredients together except the strawberries and chocolate chips. Fold well to ensure no lumps.
- Fold in strawberries and chocolate chips.
- Pour the batter into two 8 oz mason jars and cover the jars with foil.
- Place the metal trivet into the Ninja Foodi and add 1 cup of water to the bowl.
- Place the two mason jars on top of the trivet and close the pressure cooker top. Seal the steamer valve and set the timer to 10 minutes
- Let the pressure naturally release and then open the lid and enjoy the warm cake.

CALORIES: 326G, PROTEIN: 8G, CARBOHYDRATES: 35G, FAT: 18G, SODIUM: 228MG, SUGAR: 26G.

DESSERT RECIPES

Pound Cake

PREPARATION TIME 10 MINUTES | **COOKING TIME** 25 MINUTES | **SERVINGS** 12 PERSONS

Ingredients:

- 227 g butter
- 227 g sugar
- 4 large eggs room temp
- 4.9ml Vanilla Extract
- 226.8 g flour
- 1 orange zest only
- 14.18g butter for greasing pan
- 41.3g Demerara Sugar

Instructions:

- Combine butter and sugar with a stand mixer and whip with the spatula until light and fluffy. Scratch the pages every few minutes.
- Add one egg at a time and whip over low heat until just incorporated. Repeat with the remaining 3 eggs.
- Add vanilla extract and mix to work only.
- Slowly add the flour and mix in a stand mixer. Mix over low heat until all the flour is incorporated, without over-mixing.
- Add the zest of an orange and mix.
- Butter a 7 "pan in the pan. Add demerara sugar to the pan and move it to stick to the sides. Try to avoid the centre.
- Put water in the inner pot of the Ninja Foodi. Cover the cake with foil and cover a little. Put the stand in the lower position of the Ninja Foodi. Put the pressure on high for 25 minutes. Make sure the black valve is in the sealing position. When the time is up, let it loosen naturally for 20 minutes.
- When natural release ends, manually release all pressure. There may not be and the red pin is already in. Place on a cooling shelf and let cool for 5 minutes.
- Turn the cake over to the cooling rack and gently place the cake on the rack over low heat. Take the cake back to Ninja Foodi. Set Bake / Broil to 400 ° F and bake for 5 to 10 minutes or until top is golden brown.

CALORIES 365 PROTEIN 4G CARBS 36G FAT 16G FIBRE 1.2G SODIUM 170MG SUGAR 22G

DESSERT RECIPES

Onion and Smoky Mushroom Medley

PREPARATION TIME
5 MINUTES

COOKING TIME
2 MINUTES

SERVINGS
4 PERSONS

Ingredients:

- 12.19g ghee
- 1 carton button mushrooms, sliced
- 1 onion, diced
- 3g salt
- 5–10 ml coconut aminos
- 0.28g smoked paprika

Instructions:

- Set your Ninja Foodi to Sauté mode and add ghee, let it heat up
- Add mushrooms, onion and seasoning, Sauté for 5 minutes
- Lock lid and cook on high pressure for 3 minutes
- Quick release pressure
- Serve warm and enjoy!

CALORIES: 268 PROTEIN: 10G CARBOHYDRATES: 11G FAT: 20G

DESSERT RECIPES

Simple Treat of Garlic

PREPARATION TIME 10 MINUTES **COOKING TIME** 45 MINUTES **SERVINGS** 1 PERSONS

Ingredients:

- 15 ml extra-virgin olive oil
- 2 garlic cloves, minced
- 2 large-sized Belgian endive, halved lengthwise
- 125 ml apple cider vinegar
- 125 ml broth
- Salt and pepper to taste
- 5 ml cayenne pepper

Instructions:

- Set your Ninja Foodi to Sauté mode and add oil, let the oil heat up
- Add garlic and cook for 30 seconds unto browned
- Add endive, vinegar, broth, salt, pepper, and cayenne
- Lock lid and cook on low pressure for 2 minutes. Quick release pressure and serve. Enjoy!
-

CALORIES: 91 PROTEIN: 2G CARBOHYDRATES: 3G FAT: 6G

DESSERT RECIPES

Cauliflower Soup

PREPARATION TIME 10 MINUTES
COOKING TIME 30 MINUTES
SERVINGS 5 PERSONS

Ingredients:

- 5 slices bacon, chopped
- 1 onion, chopped
- 3 garlic cloves, minced
- 1 cauliflower head, trimmed
- 950 ml chicken broth
- 240 ml almond milk
- 5.9g salt
- 2.33 g black pepper
- 169.5g cheddar cheese, shredded
- Sour cream and chopped fresh chives for serving

Instructions:

- Set your pot to Sauté mode and pre-heat it for 5 minutes on high settings
- Add bacon, onion, garlic to your pot and cook for 5 minutes
- Reserve bacon for garnish
- Add cauliflower, chicken broth to the pot and place pressure cooker lid, seal the pressure valves
- Cook on high pressure for 10 minutes, quick release the pressure once did
- Add milk, and mash the soup reaches your desired consistency
- Season with salt, pepper and sprinkle cheese evenly on top of the soup
- Close crisping lid and Broil for 5 minutes
- Once done, top with reserved crispy bacon and serve with sour cream and chives. Enjoy!

CALORIES: 253 PROTEIN: 13G CARBOHYDRATES: 12G FAT: 17G

DESSERT RECIPES

Pumpkin Pie

PREPARATION TIME 5 MINUTES
COOKING TIME 10 MINUTES
SERVINGS 8 PERSONS

Ingredients:
- 3 large eggs
- 67 g sugar
- 123 g pumpkin puree
- 10 ml vanilla extract
- 3.78g pumpkin pie spice
- 182 g Single cream
- 238 g heavy whipping cream

Instructions:
- Combine eggs and sugar in a medium mixing bowl. whip until just combined.
- Add tinned pumpkin and pumpkin pie seasoning. whip until just combined.
- Add the vanilla extract, Single cream, and heavy whipped cream. whip until just combined. Mix in 8 Mason jars.
- Place the lids on the mason jars and tighten by hand. Put water in the inner pot of the Ninja Foodi.
- Put the glasses in the basket in two layers. Replace the pressure cap and turn the black valve to seal. Cook on high pressure for 7 minutes. Allow it to deflate naturally for 7 minutes, then manually release the remaining pressure.
- Take the glasses out of the basket and let them sit for about 15 minutes. Then place in the refrigerator for 4 hours.
- Top with whipped cream and pumpkin pie spice. Serve and enjoy!

CALORIES 211 PROTEIN 8G CARBS 13G FAT 16G FIBRE 1G SODIUM 58MG SUGAR 9G

DESSERT RECIPES

Dried tomatoes

PREPARATION TIME 10 MINUTES
COOKING TIME 3 HOURS
SERVINGS 1 PERSONS

Ingredients:

- 5 medium tomatoes
- 15 ml, basil
- 75 ml, organic olive oil
- 5 ml, paprika
- 5 ml, cilantro
- 15 ml, onion powder

Instructions:

- Wash the tomatoes and slice them.
- Combine cilantro with basil and paprika. Stir well.
- Place the sliced tomatoes in the pressure cooker and add the spice mixture.
- Add organic olive oil and close the lid.
- Cook the dish on slow mode for 8 hours.
- When the cooking time ends, the tomatoes should be semi-dry. Remove them from the pressure cooker.
- Serve your dried tomatoes warm.

CALORIES 92, PROTEINS 1 G, CARBOHYDRATES 3.84 G FATS 8.6 G,

DESSERT RECIPES

Paprika And Cabbage

PREPARATION TIME 10 MINUTES

COOKING TIME 20 MINUTES

SERVINGS 4-6 PERSONS

Ingredients:

- 680g green cabbage, shredded
- 250 ml vegetable stock
- 1.25 ml sweet paprika
- 45 ml ghee
- Salt to taste
- pepper as required

Instructions:

- Set your Ninja Foodi to Sauté mode and add ghee, let it melt
- Add cabbage, salt, pepper, and stock, stir well
- Lock lid and cook on high pressure for 7 minutes. Quick release pressure
- Add paprika and toss well. Divide between plates and serve. Enjoy!

CALORIES: 170 PROTEIN: 5G CARBOHYDRATES: 5G FAT: 4G

DESSERT RECIPES

Corn Dog Bites

PREPARATION TIME
10 MINUTES

COOKING TIME
10 MINUTES

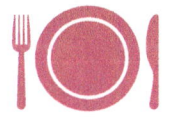

SERVINGS
14 PERSONS

Ingredients:

- 4 hot dogs cut
- 280g flour
- 96g corn Flour
- 50 g sugar
- 9.8g Bicarbonate of soda
- 3g salt
- 250 ml milk
- 1 egg
- 60 ml oil optional

Instructions:

- Combine the dry ingredients for the cornbread, then add the milk, oil and egg and mix well.
- Spray the inside of your egg mould with non-stick spray (good). Fill each pocket halfway with the cornbread mixture.
- Cut each hot dog into 4 equal pieces and press 1 piece into the centre of each hole filled with cornbread.
- Cover the egg pan with foil
- Pour 354 ml of water into your Ninja Foodi. Place the egg on a trivet with handles and lower into your pot.
- Close the lid and the steam valve and put on high pressure for 9 minutes. Then let it steam naturally for 5 minutes. Then let the rest of the steam escape.
- Immediately remove the foil and let cool in the pan for 3 to 4 minutes to keep them intact when you remove them.
- Then turn and gently squeeze the lower pockets so that every bite of corn comes out.

CALORIES 170 PROTEIN 4G CARBS 21G FAT 7G FIBRE 1G SODIUM 184MG SUGAR 4G

VEGETABLE AND SOUP RECIPES

VEGETABLE AND SOUP

Chili-quinoa 'n Black Bean Soup

PREPARATION TIME 10 MINUTES

COOKING TIME 20 MINUTES

SERVINGS 2 PERSONS

Ingredients:

- 1/2 bell pepper, diced
- 1 medium-sized sweet potatoes, peeled and diced
- 1/2 onion, diced
- 14.1g tomato paste
- 16g diced tomatoes
- 1 clove garlic, minced
- 1 stalk celery, chopped
- 312ml vegetable broth
- Salt to taste
- 22.5 g quinoa
- 475 ml vegetable broth
- 1/3 can black beans, rinsed and drained
- 2.30 g each of paprika and cumin

Instructions:

- Place all ingredients in the Ninja Foodi. Give a good stir.
- Install pressure lid.
- Close Ninja Foodi, press the pressure button, choose high settings, and set time to 20 minutes.
- Once done cooking, do a quick release.
- Serve and enjoy.

CALORIES: 377; PROTEIN: 18.1G; CARBOHYDRATES: 73.7G; FAT: 1.0G

VEGETABLE AND SOUP

Vegan Chili

PREPARATION TIME 10 MINUTES
COOKING TIME 50 MINUTES
SERVINGS 8 PERSONS

Ingredients:

- 5 ml olive oil
- 1 medium onion, diced
- 3 cloves garlic, minced
- 1 tinned crushed tomato
- 237ml vegetable broth
- 4 large carrots, chopped (about 180 g)
- 5 stalks celery, chopped (about 180 g)
- 164g corn kernels
- 18g tamari
- 8.13g chili powder, added to taste
- salt and black pepper to taste
- 3 medium russet potatoes, chopped (about 380g)
- 256 g cooked kidney beans
- 256 g cooked black beans

Instructions:

- Select sear / sauté in Ninja Foodi and set MD: HI. Preheat for 5 minutes.
- Add olive oil, onion and garlic to the pot and sauté for 5 minutes, stirring occasionally, until lightly browned.
- Add the rest of the ingredients (except the cornbread dough) to the pot.
- Install the pressure plug and make sure the drain valve is in the seal position. Select pressure and set high. Set the time to 15 minutes and select start / stop to start.
- When pressure cooking is complete, quickly release the valve by moving the pressure relief valve to the vent position. Carefully remove the cap when the device is depressurized.
- Stir the chili quickly. Use a spoon to pour about half of the Mini Muffin Vegan Cornbread Dough over the chili pepper (see note in Vegan Cornbread Recipe for what to do with leftover dough).
- Close the lid to grill. Select bake / roast, set the temperature to 191ºC and the time to 12 minutes. Select start / stop to begin.

CALORIES 438 PROTEIN 27.9G CARBS 87.3G FAT 3.5G FIBRE 31.4G SODIUM 535MG SUGAR 11.2G

VEGETABLE AND SOUP

Mashed Potatoes

PREPARATION TIME 15 MINUTES   **COOKING TIME** 15 MINUTES   **SERVINGS** 8 PERSONS

Ingredients:

- 1361g Yukon Gold or Russet Potatoes, Peeled and Quartered
- 250 ml Water
- 120 g Cream
- 62g Sour Cream
- 56.7g Unsalted Butter
- 6g Garlic Salt or to Taste

Instructions:

- Take the peeled and quartered potatoes and place them in the Ninja Foodi.
- Add 1 cup of water.
- Put the pressure cooker lid on the Ninja Foodi and secure it making sure the spout is "sealed".
- Cook under high pressure for 10 minutes using the pressure cooker function.
- Steam naturally 5 minutes after cooking time (do nothing).
- After 5 minutes, quickly release the steam, then remove the lid.
- Using a silicone potato masher, carefully mash the potatoes in the pan.
- Add the rest of the ingredients and toss to combine the potatoes.
- Close the lid attached to the Ninja Foodi and cook at 350 degrees for 3 minutes.
- Open the lid and serve.

CALORIES 238 PROTEIN 4G CARBS 27G FAT 12G FIBRE 3G SODIUM 154MG SUGAR 2G

VEGETABLE AND SOUP

Spinach and Chickpea Stew

PREPARATION TIME 10 MINUTES

COOKING TIME 25 MINUTES

SERVINGS 8 PERSONS

Ingredients:

- 17.7 ml extra-virgin olive oil
- 1 yellow onion, diced 4 garlic cloves, minced
- 4 sweet potatoes, peeled and diced
- 950 ml vegetable broth
- 1 tin (400 g) fire-roasted diced tomatoes, drained
- 2 tins (425 g) each chickpea, drained
- 2.58g ground coriander
- 1.15g paprika
- 3g salt
- 1.17g fresh ground black pepper
- 120g spinach

Instructions:

- Add the oil, onion and garlic to the pot, stir and cook for 5 minutes.
- Then add the sweet potatoes, vegetable broth, tomatoes, chickpeas, cumin, coriander, paprika, salt and pepper to the Ninja Foodi pot. Replace the cap and close the pressure valves. Cook on high for 8 minutes.
- Quickly release the pressure and add the spinach to the pot.
- Stir until tender. Enjoy!
- Serve the Chickpea Stew with rice

CALORIES 166 PROTEIN 5.9G CARBS 29.7G FAT 2.9G FIBRE 7G SODIUM 605MG SUGAR 3.2G

VEGETABLE AND SOUP

Vegetable tart

PREPARATION TIME 5 MINUTES

COOKING TIME 10 MINUTES

SERVINGS 4 PERSONS

Ingredients:

- 200g puff pastry
- 1 egg yolk
- 2 red bell peppers
- 1 red onion
- 1 eggplant
- 5 ml ground black
- 140g tomatoes
- pepper as required
- 15 ml turmeric
- 200g goat cheese
- 60 ml cream
- 85g zucchini
- 5 ml salt
- 5 ml olive oil

Instructions:

- Whisk the egg yolk, combine it with the ground black pepper and stir well.
- Roll the puff pastry using a rolling pin. Spray the pressure cooker with the olive oil inside and add the puff pastry.
- Spread the puff pastry with the whisked egg. Chop the tomatoes and dice the onions. Chop the eggplants and zucchini.
- Combine the vegetables together and sprinkle them with the salt, turmeric, and cream. Mix well and place the vegetable mixture in the pressure cooker.
- Chop the red bell peppers and sprinkle the pressure cooker mixture with them. Grate the goat cheese and sprinkle the tart with the cheese.
- Close the pressure cooker lid Cook at Pressure mode for 25 minutes. When the dish is cooked, release the pressure and open the pressure cooker lid. Check if the tart is cooked and remove it from the pressure cooker.
- Cut the tart into slices and serve it.

CALORIES 279, PROTEIN 10 G, CARBOHYDRATES 18.42 G, FATS 18.8 G,

VEGETABLE AND SOUP

Sweet sriracha carrots

PREPARATION TIME 10 MINUTES

COOKING TIME 40 MINUTES

SERVINGS 2 PERSONS

Ingredients:

- 30 ml sriracha
- 250 ml of water
- 5 ml Erythritol
- 30 ml olive oil
- 125 ml dill
- 450g carrots
- 5 ml oregano

Instructions:

- Wash the carrots, peel them, and slice them. Set the pressure cooker to Sauté mode. Pour the olive oil into the pressure cooker and add the sliced carrots.
- Sprinkle the vegetables with the oregano and dill. Sauté the dish for 15 minutes, stirring frequently.
- Sprinkle the carrot with Erythritol, water, and sriracha. Mix well.
- Close the pressure cooker lid and cook the dish on Pressure mode for 2 minutes.
- When the cooking time ends, release the remaining pressure and open the pressure cooker lid. Transfer the carrots to a serving plate.

CALORIES 74, PROTEIN 1.2G CARBOHYDRATES 9.3G, FAT 4.2G,

VEGETABLE AND SOUP

Cauliflower puree with scallions

PREPARATION TIME
10 MINUTES

COOKING TIME
15 MINUTES

SERVINGS
6 PERSONS

Ingredients:

- 1 head cauliflower
- 85g scallions
- 15 ml salt
- 60 ml butter
- 1.25 ml sesame seeds
- 1 egg yolk
- 1 litre of water
- 5 ml chicken stock

Instructions:

- Wash the cauliflower and chop it roughly. Place the cauliflower in the pressure cooker.
- Add the water and salt. Close the pressure cooker lid and cook the vegetables on Pressure mode for 5 minutes.
- Release the pressure and open the pressure cooker lid. Remove the cauliflower from the pressure cooker and let it rest briefly.
- Place the cauliflower in a blender. Add the butter, chicken stock, and sesame seeds. Blend the mixture well.
- Chop the scallions. Add the egg yolk to the blender and blend the mixture for 30 seconds. Remove the cauliflower puree from the blender and combine it with the scallions.
- Mix well and serve.

CALORIES 94, PROTEIN 2 G CARBOHYDRATES 3.39 G, FATS 8.7 G,

VEGETABLE AND SOUP

Chickpea and Potato Soup

PREPARATION TIME 10 MINUTES
COOKING TIME 15 MINUTES
SERVINGS 2 PERSONS

Ingredients:

- 14.79ml olive oil
- ½ onion, chopped
- 3 cloves of garlic, minced
- 100 g chopped tomato
- 6 ml fennel space
- 1.2g onion powder
- 0.82g garlic powder
- 26g oregano
- 0.66g cinnamon
- 0.46g thyme
- 1 large potato, peeled and cubed
- 40 g carrots, chopped
- 253g cooked chickpeas
- 237 ml water
- 240 ml almond milk
- 67 g kale, chopped
- Salt to taste
- pepper as required

Instructions:

- Press the sauté button on the Ninja Foodi and sauté the onion and garlic until fragrant.
- Stir in the tomatoes, fennel, onion powder, garlic powder, oregano, cinnamon, and thyme. Stir until well-combined.
- Add the rest of the ingredients. Install pressure lid. Close Ninja Foodi, press the pressure button, choose high settings, and set time to 10 minutes.
- Once done cooking, do a quick release. Serve and enjoy.

CALORIES: 543; PROTEIN: 17.7G; CARBOHYDRATES: 91.0G; FAT: 12G

VEGETABLE AND SOUP

Black beans in tomato sauce

PREPARATION TIME 10 MINUTES

COOKING TIME 15-20 MINUTES

SERVINGS 4 PERSONS

Ingredients:

- 225g black beans
- 1 onion
- 250 ml tomato paste
- 15 ml minced garlic
- 5 ml ground black pepper
- 115g celery stalk
- 1 litre chicken stock
- 2.5 ml chilli pepper
- 2.5 ml turmeric

Instructions:

- Place the black beans in the pressure cooker. Peel the onion and chop it. Add the tomato paste, garlic, ground black pepper.
- Chicken stock chilli pepper and turmeric in the pressure cooker. Mix well and close the pressure cooker lid.
- Cook the dish on Pressure mode for 15 minutes. When the cooking time ends, release the pressure and open the pressure cooker lid.
- Add the chopped onion and mix well. Close the pressure cooker lid and cook the dish on Sauté mode for 4 minutes.
- Open the pressure cooker lid and mix well. Transfer the cooked dish to a serving bowl.

CALORIES 109, PROTEIN 6 G, CARBOHYDRATES 17.59 G, FATS 2.1 G,

VEGETABLE AND SOUP

Roasted veggie mix

PREPARATION TIME 15 MINUTES   **COOKING TIME** 15 MINUTES   **SERVINGS** 6 PERSONS

Ingredients:

- 2 eggplants
- 2 bell peppers
- 2 turnips
- 1 zucchini
- 15 ml salt
- 225g tomatoes
- 45 ml sesame oil
- 1 litre beef broth
- 15 ml oregano
- 2 carrots

Instructions:

- Peel the eggplants and chop them. Sprinkle the eggplants with the salt and stir well. Remove the seeds from the bell peppers and chop them.
- Slice the tomatoes and chop turnips. Chop the zucchini.
- Peel the carrots and grate them. Transfer all the vegetables to the pressure cooker. Add the oregano, sesame oil, and beef broth.
- Mix well and close the pressure cooker lid. Cook the dish on Steam mode for 30 minutes.
- When the cooking time ends, transfer the dish to serving bowls.

CALORIES 107, PROTEIN 4 G CARBOHYDRATES 13.2 G, FATS 5 G,

VEGETABLE AND SOUP

Pressure Cooker Chicken Pot Pie Soup

PREPARATION TIME
17 MINUTES

COOKING TIME
17 MINUTES

SERVINGS
6 PERSONS

Ingredients:

- 1 large skinless boneless chicken breast, bite-size cubed
- 1 can drained Libby's mixed vegetables
- 13.7 g olive oil
- 3.6g of garlic salt
- 8.62 g minced garlic
- 375 ml chicken broth
- 231g whipping double cream
- 24.36 g corn-starch
- 18g chicken broth or cold water
- 1 refrigerated biscuits tube

Instructions:

- Sauté chicken with garlic, olive oil, and garlic salt.
- Then add broth and veggie mix and stir. Pressure cooks for two minutes at high.
- Add cream and mix cornstarch with water or broth. Add gradually and let it get dense for two minutes.
- Place the biscuit dough over upside-down tin for the muffin. Bake for about 11 minutes and serve soup in them.

CALORIES: 546 PROTEIN: 16G CARBS: 52G FAT: 31G

VEGETABLE AND SOUP

Gentle and Simple Fish Stew

PREPARATION TIME 5 MINUTES

COOKING TIME 20 MINUTES

SERVINGS 4 PERSONS

Ingredients:

- 700 ml fish stock
- 1 onion, diced
- 71g broccoli, chopped
- 2 celery stalks, chopped
- 102g cauliflower, diced
- 1 carrot, sliced
- 453.59g white fish fillets, chopped
- 231g double cream
- 1 bay leaf
- 28.35g butter
- 1.42 g pepper
- 3 g salt
- 0.82g garlic powder

Instructions:

- Set your Ninja Foodi to "Sauté" mode and add butter, let it melt.
- Add onion and carrots, cook for 3 minutes.
- Stir in remaining ingredients.
- Lock the lid and cook on high pressure for 4 minutes.
- Naturally, release the pressure over 10 minutes.
- Discard bay leaf.
- Serve and enjoy!

CALORIES: 298 PROTEIN: 24 G CARBOHYDRATES: 6 G FAT: 18 G

VEGETABLE AND SOUP

Creamy Early Morning Asparagus Soup

PREPARATION TIME 10 MINUTES
COOKING TIME 20 MINUTES
SERVINGS 4 PERSONS

Ingredients:

- 13.3g olive oil
- 3 green onions, sliced crosswise
- 453.59g asparagus, tough ends removed, cut into 1-inch pieces
- 950ml vegetable stock
- 14.2g unsalted butter
- 6 g almond flour
- 11.38 g salts
- 2.40 g white pepper
- 120 g double cream

Instructions:

- Set your Ninja Foodi to "Sauté" mode and add oil, let it heat up
- Add green onions and Sauté for a few minutes, add asparagus and stock
- Lock lid and cook on high pressure for 5 minutes
- Take a small saucepan and place it over low heat, add butter, flour and stir until the mixture foams and turns into a golden beige, this is your blond roux
- Remove from heat
- Release pressure naturally over 10 minutes
- Open lid and add roux, salt and pepper to the soup
- Use an immersion blender to puree the soup
- Taste and season accordingly, swirl in cream and enjoy!

CALORIES 192, PROTEIN 6G CARBOHYDRATES 8G FAT 14G

VEGETABLE AND SOUP

Beef Sausage Soup

PREPARATION TIME 10 MINUTES
COOKING TIME 30 MINUTES
SERVINGS 6 PERSONS

Ingredients:

- 14.79 ml extra-virgin olive oil
- 1,419.5ml beef broth
- 8 organic beef sausage, cooked and sliced
- 284g sauerkraut
- 2 celery stalks, chopped
- 1 sweet onion, chopped
- 6.56 g garlic, minced
- 28.35 g butter
- 15.79 g hot mustard
- 2.28 g caraway seeds
- 123 g sour cream
- 3.24 g fresh parsley, chopped

Instructions:

- Grease the inner pot of your Ninja Foodi with olive oil.
- Add broth, sausage, sauerkraut, celery, onion, garlic, butter, mustard, caraway seeds in the pot.
- Lock the lid and cook on high pressure for 30 minutes.
- Quick-release the pressure.
- Remove the lid and stir in sour cream.
- Serve with a topping of parsley.
- Enjoy!

CALORIES: 165 PROTEIN: 11 G CARBOHYDRATES: 14 G. FAT: 4 G

VEGETABLE AND SOUP

Broccoli casserole

PREPARATION TIME 10 MINUTES

COOKING TIME 45 MINUTES

SERVINGS 6 PERSONS

Ingredients:

- 280g broccoli
- 250 ml cream
- 200g mushrooms
- 1 onion
- 1 bell pepper
- 125 ml chicken stock
- 225g crackers
- 15 ml butter
- 5 ml ground black pepper
- 15 ml salt
- 75 ml green peas

Instructions:

- Chop the broccoli and slice the mushrooms. Crush the crackers and combine them with the ground black pepper and stir well.
- Chop the bell pepper and onion. Place the broccoli in the pressure cooker. Make a layer with the bell pepper and onion.
- Combine the cream and salt together. Stir the mixture and add the green peas.
- Pour the cream mixture in the pressure cooker. Add chicken stock and butter. Sprinkle the casserole mixture with the crushed crackers.
- Close the pressure cooker lid and cook the dish on Sauté mode for 25 minutes.
- When the cooking time ends, let the dish rest briefly before serving.

CALORIES 317, PROTEIN 7 G CARBOHYDRATES 41.89 G, FATS 15.4 G,

CONCLUSION

You have completed your first step to culinary freedom. You can now cook in an unheated kitchen.

The next step from here is to explore even further and find your own culinary footing! Learn the basics from this recipes, and come up with your very own awesome Ninja Foodi Friendly recipes and make your ultimate meal plan!

The Ninja Foodi possesses the unique ability to micro-wave food, so if you are looking for a one-stop-shop for your food-cooking needs, it really doesn't get any better than the Ninja Foodi! You see, with just one appliance, you will be able to make the staples of your diet! You will be able to make rice, soup, stews, pastas, deep fried foods, and vegetable dishes, all with the simple touch of a button! So, what you are telling yourself at. This is far too good to be true! I know, I know! Of course, the question on your mind would definitely be: how can the Ninja Foodi deliver such great attributes for such a low price? Instead of having to spend over a hundred dollars on a rice cooker, a slow cooker, and an air fryer, the Ninja Foodi has all of those functions in one tiny, inexpensive appliance. Not only does it have those attributes, but it is able to take your cooking to the next level. Now, you can make the most delicious steamed or deep fried foods in your own home! Your whole family will be motivated to eat clean and more often, all because you singlehandedly took control of your kitchen! Lastly, if you feel like your Ninja Foodi is just not up to snuff, don't worry! Ninja Foodi is not like any other appliance that you will probably ever encounter. A Ninja Foodist always trusts and follows their instincts, and you should too. The Ninja Foodist rewards us for doing so. Ninja Foodist that is what we ninja's are training to become. If you look at the Ninja Foodi Cam you'll notice that it is almost the same size as the Ninja Foodi itself, but for ninja training purposes we must use the Cam to train our reflexes. Just like one must when learning to use a silent but deadly weapon like the Shurikon. A Ninja Foodist learns to be able to respond to any situation in a relatively quick manner, and when training like this, we must do so much faster than ever before. Like Ninja Foodist's already do, we must do so while dealing with a situation on a much larger scale.

Fire is still a big deal, so keep on practicing … please. Try to avoid meat or fish in most of your meals, or you'll get massive heartburn. Enjoy your Ninja Cooking skills! It is fun to create new recipes and experiment. You don't need a microwave, just add foil, aluminum foil, etc to your dishes to be heated. Making beans in your Ninja Cooking is great. Since they are very water soluble, they will add their own water to your dish when you cook them. Plates, bowls, baking sheets and glass will work just as well as induction cooktops or a non-microwave

Printed in Great Britain
by Amazon